I0829669

The

Centennial Anniversary

Anthology

of

The Poetry Society of Virginia

2023

Published by High Tide Publications, Inc.
Deltaville, Virginia
www.HighTidePublications.com

Printed in the United States of America.

ISBN 978-1-945990-99-1 - First Edition

*****

About the Cover:

Crim Dell: In the early 1960s, W&M planned to build a library on the site of Crim Dell. When plans changed and Swem Library was built near the middle of the campus, President Pascall presided over the official dedication of Crim Dell in May, 1966. The area is named in memory of John W. H. Crim, 1901. The Crim Dell Bridge was a gift to the College from the Class of 1964. According to campus lore, two people who cross the bridge holding hands will be lifelong friends, and if they kiss, lifetime lovers.
In 1997, the bridge was declared unsafe and in need of repairs. It was closed for repairs and, due to codes in force, was made not only safer but handicap accessible. The bridge survived the construction without losing its classic beauty, and was reopened in 1998.
Photo by: Jeanne Hopke W&M Class of 1980

Etching Page ii - Jeanne Johansen

Table of Contents

The Poetry Society of Virginia
Centennial Anthology
Development Committee

PSV President

Terry Cox-Joseph

Committee Chairman

Edward W. Lull

Editor-in-Chief

Edward W. Lull

Co-Editors

Carolyn Kreiter-Foronda
Sofia M. Starnes

Committee Members (Poets Laureate of Virginia)

Carolyn Kreiter-Foronda (2006-2008)
Sofia M. Starnes (2012-2014)
Ron Smith (2014-2016)
Henry Hart (2018-2020)
Luisa A. Igloria (2020-2022)

Sir Christopher Wren Building
College of William and Mary
Williamsburg, Virginia

Site of the founding of
The Poetry Society of Virginia
May 1923

The Poetry Society of Virginia, 1923-2023

Preface

Most contemporary poets have heard of such literary greats as Robert Frost and Edna St. Vincent Millay, but one thing we don't often connect with them is the dates of their fame. 1923 was the year The Poetry Society of Virginia was founded. Among the first visiting poets were Frost and Millay. Our founders, including our first president, Dr. Charles Feidelson, were big thinkers. Nothing like starting at the top.

Consider other greats who rose to fame in 1923: T.S. Eliot, D.H. Lawrence, William Butler Yeats, e. e. cummings, Robert Frost, Wallace Stevens, William Carlos Williams, Jean Cocteau, Pablo Neruda, Edgar Allan Poe, and Rainer Maria Rilke. Imagine Edna St. Vincent Millay receiving her Pulitzer Prize just three years after she received the right to vote.

In 1923, there were no computers, no Zoom meetings, no PayPal accounts. There was postal service, and there were telephones. If only Feidelson and that founding group could see us now. What would they think of contemporary poetry? Of Allen Ginsberg, Claudia Emerson, Natasha Trethewey, Jericho Brown? Surely there would be debate about forms—free verse and spoken word—as there is today. Or whether forms should be combined, such as blues and sonnets, or tankas alternating with stanzas in villanelles.

Overall though, I like to think that our founders, open-minded as they were, would recognize both the diminution and the growth of poetry today. What we have lost through texting and TikTok we have gained through the birth in many poems, akin to e. e. cummings's lower case and lightheartedness. Despite the loss of readership of weighty novels (think Tolstoy), we are experiencing a rise in pre-teen and young-adult readership, particularly in the realm of fantasy (think J.K. Rowling), as well as an explosion of fantasy-vampire-SF poetry. Not to mention flash poetry. Frustrating as our abbreviated, truncated, mutilated language and attention spans may be, they provide the opportunity to create "elevator speeches," to compress and distill concepts and philosophical musings into bite-size pieces that can be studied at leisure. These "gotcha" platforms, while catering to short attention spans, might yet encourage our pinpoint focus on topics we might not consider otherwise. We live with that hope; we endeavor to make it a reality.

This brings us to the issue of growth in The Poetry Society of Virginia. Not knowing how many members the PSV's founders expected to bring in that first year, I hope that our increasing numbers across the state, one hundred years later, would please them. As of 2022, we are four hundred strong, with about fifteen percent of us from outside Virginia. While the Christopher Wren Chapel symbolizes our origins, the state of Virginia and beyond are our actuality—and our potential. Perhaps a Space-X rocket could be Photoshopped onto our webpage cover photo.

We strive for inclusion. And we strive for growth through our youth. This means encouraging self-expression in our students, as well as introducing them to traditional forms and to the poets who preceded us. From these luminaries, each generation learns that poetry deals with a wide range of emotions: heartbreak, loss, grief and joy, departures and returns, our shared and complex history, the feeling of being an outsider, the plight and the bonds of marginalized groups. All that and more. United States Poet Laureate, Joy Harjo, who was appointed three times to that role by the Library of Congress, once wrote: "Remember the sky that you were born under,/know each of the star's stories. … /Remember the earth whose skin you are:/red earth, black earth, yellow earth, white earth/brown earth, we are earth./Remember all is in motion, is growing, is you./ Remember language comes from this./Remember the dance language is, that life is./ Remember."

In one sense, our mission has remained the same. "The Poetry Society of Virginia seeks to promote the writing and enjoyment of poetry through a wide range of programs and monthly events, offered in five regions across Virginia." While the number of regions continually changes with fluctuations in the population, the reach of our message continues to expand. Since its inception, the Society has developed numerous outreach activities that go beyond readings and presentations. One example is the Young Poets in the Community program. High school and college students are paid a stipend to represent poetry in their school and home communities. We believe it's an effective way of involving students and of keeping poetry alive, both in written and spoken form. In addition to writing poetry, these young people learn to network and perform their work, and they take on the responsibility of reporting back to the Society, keeping us informed of their work and accomplishments.

Another example of our growth is the implementation of the annual PSV North American Book Award. Publishers and authors are invited to submit books published in the preceding year, and each submission is accompanied by an entry fee which subsidizes the contest, including its $1,000 prize (as of 2022). While running the contest entails a considerable amount of work, the benefits of sponsoring the award are multifold: committee members read cutting-edge, high-quality poetry by newly published poets; PSV members are encouraged by the winners' successes to have their own work published by discerning publishers; through newspaper and online announcements, the general public sees not only the poet's name, but also that of our society; the winning poets receive publicity and financial compensation, in an experience that we hope will lead to a strong bond with the PSV. More importantly, the award is a tangible evidence of our support of poets and of the presses that publish their work.

Our Annual Spring Festival, held at William and Mary, where the Society was founded, is a fun, energizing, educational event, as well as an in-person opportunity for networking and book sales. It brings in top talent, including professors, performers, and nationally known poets. Attendees and supporters come from across the country, often spending a night or two in the area in order to explore Colonial Williamsburg and the Historic Triangle with their families. As a special bonus, the Festival features a reading by the winner of the year's North American Book Award.

As the Society grows, so do our needs, particularly in regard to people willing to engage in the task of lifting up poets and poetry, often through practical means. We rely on talented volunteers adept at networking, accounting, organizing— people who can manage and judge the many contests we sponsor, who are willing to share new ideas and are ready to help implement them. So, please join us in celebrating our 100th year. Join us by reading the poems in this collection. They represent a cross-section of our members' work over the last century: the joys, the angst, the beauty, the questions, the histories, the ethnicities, the talent. From nature to life and death, from fortitude to despair, our members write of what matters to them, and those topics contain universal themes. Savor their form, content, and spirit. Join us—and enjoy.

Terry Cox-Joseph
President, The Poetry Society of Virginia

From the Editor's Desk

Building a book like this takes a significant amount of time, effort, and patience, but what a joy it has been. I was privileged to have Carolyn Kreiter-Foronda and Sofia Starnes, both former Poets Laureate of Virginia, as teammates through the more difficult phases of the endeavor: collecting, reviewing, selecting, editing, and assembling the manuscript. Also, I relied on the backing and support of PSV President, Terry Cox-Joseph, who wrote the Preface, an important ingredient of the book. The expertise and guidance of our publisher, Jeanne Johansen, of High Tide Publications, would take us successfully across the finish line.

The Centennial Anthology contains several sections. Part One consists of the poetry of 110 contemporary poets, while Part Two features poems by 36 poets from six previous PSV anthologies. The four appendices provide (A) information regarding previous PSV Presidents, (B) the contributions of the various Poets Laureate of Virginia, (C) brief biographies of the participating poets, and (D) acknowledgments of prior publication of the poems. The Table of Contents lists the poets alphabetically.

When preparing the proposal for the development of this anthology, to be published by the centennial date of May 2023, I had to make sure I used the proper title of the organization. Two titles appear in official and non-official documents over the years: *The Poetry Society of Virginia* and *Poetry Society of Virginia*. The use—or omission—of an article may seem like a small thing, but it is not trivial, if the book is to be a correct and consistent representation of the Society for the next one hundred years, at least. And so, I turned to previous anthologies for guidance, only to find a mixed usage there, too. But when I got to the first two anthologies I uncovered still another mystery. The first collection, dated 1932, was titled *Lyric Virginia To-Day*; the second, published in 1956, was titled *Lyric Virginia To-Day, Vol.2*. Neither volume made reference to The Poetry Society of Virginia or PSV on the dust cover, the hard cover, the title page, or anywhere else in the books. It seems I was back where I had started. As I scratched my head, a light bulb popped on. I pulled out the By-Laws of the Society and read: *ARTICLE 1. NAME. The name of this organization shall be The Poetry Society of Virginia.* Problem solved, even though the mystery remains. Perhaps someone reading this introduction will shed some light on this unresolved segment of PSV history.

I hope that all who pick up this book will drink deeply of the beauty, talent, and creativity that our poets have placed at your disposal. We are proud to have it represent a poetic standard for the next one hundred years of The Poetry Society of Virginia.

Edward W. Lull
Editor

The Poetry Society of Virginia

The
Centennial Anniversary Anthology

1923 - 2023

Part One

Poems by Contemporary Poets

Obelia Akanke

The Light that Shines in You

When I look at you,
I see:
the manifestation of a thousand generations,
the hope a grandmother had that her descendant would have it easier than she,
the answered prayer that an ancestor's legacy would thrive in you.

I see:
the strength in wished-for tomorrows
of broken nations who slaved under the deadly heat of summer,
the root of resilience that, when exposed to the elements, still survived bitter winters.

Though villages were raided,
families torn asunder,
languages banned,
and traditions outlawed,
the core light refused to be extinguished.
We believed that you would one day exist.

And exist you shall.

The world had counted you out,
but I calculate that you are, statistically, an anomaly,
prepared and protected by God Himself.
You are the product of everyone who came before you.
We wait with bated breath
to discover how you will impact the world.

If you could see:
the circle of love that surrounds you,
relatives who've gone to glory and watch from Heaven saying, "That's my heir,"
that your very existence is a blessing,

maybe you would understand why I smile when I look at you.

You walk in the present
carrying treasures of the past
and are destined to shape the future.

You are the jewel who was predicted.

Feel it.
Embrace it.

Own it.

I offer you my support and the love of the family line that connects us to your heart.
Go forth, my daughter, and let your light shine for all to see.

Near to You

I wake up
with your name on my lips
and fall asleep
with your voice in my ear.
You star in my dreams,
and I long just to be near
you. Come closer.
Hold me
like your life depends on it.
I've breathed in your essence,
and I wanna binge on it.
Day
…night
…morning
…evening…
Time
    has no hold on me.
It
    doesn't control me.
I
measure my activities,
my work, and my tasks
by the amount of sunshine elapsed
since you last
passed
by me
…or came to stand
    beside me.

…when you last
    kissed me.
…when you last
    touched me.
Distance isn't a deterrent.
Call me. I'm coming.
I'm calm when you see me,
but inside I'm running.
Running

mentally and emotionally.
I'll be there in a second.

My heart
beats me there
because my one and only has beckoned.
You called me, Dear?
Do you need me?
Oh, I understand.
You needed to see me.
As did I you.
And being this near to you
makes it all…worth…while.

Angela Anselmo

Cheese and Apples

After all this time
we still trade thoughts
hear each other's hopes
ease each other's hurts
as good friends do.

But, I haven't forgotten—

you said it was my funny
lacy gloves that attracted
your attention that first day
we met, at your party.

You've told me since—

you really thought
those gloves ridiculous, but
being curious and polite
you admired them.

So we chatted about such trivia.
Now that we trust one another
with all the facets of our reality

I want to tell you—

it was cheese cubes on toothpicks
set into apple halves
that *intrigued* me.

I raved about your clever offering.
Your guests ate them up and
you played host to the hilt.

Of course you feigned modesty
while relishing all the praise
and I knew even then
that you and I were
cheese and apples.

April J. Asbury

Snowdrop in the Supermarket at Midnight

Glass doors slide closed, sealing
me in the chilled air; everything dying
is perfectly preserved. Metal bins
gleam, and a gloss of water
glistens on green plastic turf.

Fruit is piled like promises: pale orbs
of honeydew, mesh bags of limes. The curve
of a cantaloupe crackles like a potter's glaze,
and persimmons burn dim crimson
beside the dignified lumber of plantains.

I heft the fleshy gold of oranges,
bright tangerines, bastard tangelos,
baroque and burnished pomegranates,
the jumbled purple plums. There is no red
more red than cherries studded
with crystal, no yellow brighter
than the panes of pineapple,
no blue more otherworldly
than frosted globes of grapes.

And in that moment, I would trade
the whole waxy rainbow
for one crisp winesap,
dappled with sun, sugared
with September, its white flesh
sweeter than honey in the mouth.

The True Story of Eric's Head

I wouldn't have hit him in the head with that jar
if he hadn't begged me to do it. The boy whined—*do it,*
just do it, hit me hard.
                     It was empty, that mayo jar
mummified in masking tape, strips stained
brown to look like the woven wood
of every salad bowl at every Red Lobster
from every special dinner of the 1980s, a Bible School
craft, meant for drawing lots or holding flowers.

That's no excuse. The truth is, I hit him.

A single soft tap. He laughed, red-faced. *Harder!*
For real! That's nothing! So I hit him
hard enough to hear a soft thunk, like a boat
drifting slow and solid against the dock. *Again!*
Still laughing, grinning. *You hit like a girl!* So I hit him,
landed that jar loud and solid against his gourd,
and he swaggered off. Still laughing, still grinning,
master of jar and masking tape and his own skull.

So I was surprised (not really surprised)
when, hours later, he clambered into his mother's arms,
and tears rolled down his flushed face. His mommy rocked
and shushed him, and he bawled, snot-nosed, *She hit me,*
she hit me. She hit me in the head with a jar!

All swagger, all grinning gone. *No,* I said
to his flushed red face. *No,* I said, to his shushing
mother. *I did not,* I said, and I'd never told
a lie more bald, nor ever would, save one.
I was a good girl, but I could see it all:
he'd caught me by my pride. And even then
I knew, one day, I would tell this story.

Bill Ayres

Exposure: You and You and You Again

That photo of a maple leaf
in black and white by Ansel Adams,
the image so crisp I am sure I could cut an apple
on its serrated edge.

Such clarity, such depth,
because it was exposed to light
over and over on top of itself.

I think of our marriage,
how our years together
contribute to what we have now.

I'm amazed every day
how knowing each other's stories,
most of them, anyway,
we still have so much to tell each other.

What did you say? Lean close.
You say it isn't important.
To me it is. It is to me.

Short Order
For John Tribble

No matter how hard I scrubbed my hands
They stank from the onions I sliced.
When I ate chocolate cake
My fork was never long enough.
If I scratched my face
I had to live with that odor.
But I loved the sizzle,
The clatter of plates,
Cracking eggs, flipping burgers.
I had burns on the crook of my arm,
On my thumb, my belly,
But I loved the blue flames of the stove,
The red glow of the oven.
I loved most of the smells.
The bustle of it,
Waitresses rushing in and out.
The idea of people who came in hungry
Eating what I had made,
Wiping their chins, drinking,
Talking, at ease in their booths,
Through those swinging doors.

ZEINA AZZAM

FAR SIDE OF THE MOON
"Her face is as beautiful as the moon." Old Arab saying

She is my mother
though the nugget
of who she used to be
is now turned away from us
like the far side of the moon,
reflecting light somewhere else.

My mother pauses at
now-elusive words,
forgets how to do simple things
like changing the TV channel,
making coffee,
reading more than a few lines
of a library book.

We talk every day about
the same things
and reminisce, too, because
she loves to remember her life
before the moon shifted.

My mother is slowly letting go
of her things—the pans and spatulas
left behind like disinvited guests,
the dough hook and wire whip,
laborers for decades,
reluctantly given away.
Stained glass butterflies hovering
on her living room window
have alighted elsewhere.

Left in cabinets now are pieces
she can't forsake. Tapestries and
bowls from Palestine that remind her
of scarlet poppies, a cobalt blue sea.

An oversize tin box stuffed with
black and white photographs
from before the war,
a sentry for her memories.

She has not let go of that war—
but the war doesn't linger much
anymore on her lips
because my mother now ends
conversations before it's time,
gives up on finishing a sentence.

Yet her cratered face,
still beautiful, is illumined
by visits of a grandchild,
telephone calls, a son's embrace.
We bring chocolates, elicit a smile
that lingers a while.
My mother reminds us
to look for the moon,
even if turned, even if dark.

Hugging the Tree

> "Social distancing during Covid means no hugs." NBC News

It was neither part of a protest
nor a statement to the world.
I simply put my arms around
a tall oak and stood in embrace,
our bodies juxtaposed.
There was no swaying: her
trunk, solid and true, felt like
an ancestor, a pillar thick
with years. Her bark scratched
my skin if I moved, so I stayed
still. It was a time to be calm
and reflect on our presence
together. To look up to the sky
and fathom the height of my
partner. To inhale the earthy
scent. To arc my grateful arms
around this strong matriarch
and whisper into the wood
my wordless secret: I have not
hugged anyone for months,
my dear tree.

Madalin Jackson Bickel

Collapse of the Silver Bridge

She sparkled in the early morning sun
A jewel that spanned the ochred way,
The hazardous Ohio's muddy flow.
Aluminum and steel suspended high.
Above the concrete pillars, traffic passed
The busy life along route thirty-five.
Her soul was in the bedrock deep; her life
Held in the chains; an artery of trade,
A sign of things to come. A day for crowds
To shop then gaily head for home across
The silver span upon the fifteenth day.

No one imagined in the pouring rain
Of Cornstalk's hand upon the eyebar's pin.
A crack, a slip, and then a sonic boom.
The western deck began to fold and bend.
It shuttered, dipped, released its heavy load
That tumbled down toward an icy grave.
The twisting towers crumpled soaring down
While bodies mixed with Christmas gifts and bobbed
Like ghostly heads. A curse or flawed design?
That met with fate to meld within our minds
The memories of superstitious times.

Brown-Eyed World

No one ever said
I had Mama's eyes;
no one ever said
I had Daddy's eyes, either.
Truth be told
Aunt Wanda looked the
most like me.
At least there was
evidence I was
related by
blood....

When your mama passes,
all sorts of crazy
memories jump into
your head, flash across your
eyes like a movie
preview in reverse.
Those memories
tempted me to look back;
revisit the past, but
why?

What if my blue eyes
didn't belong in our
brown-eyed family?
Mirrors don't lie,
families do.

Patsy Anne Bickerstaff

Tour Guide. Rhine River Cruise

"This was the hill," he said. "The camps were here—and here."
His arm sweeps left to right, eyes follow; he goes on:
"The night of Christmas Eve—they all were hungry, tired,
had marched all day, knew gravely what they had to do.
but it could wait until the sun rose. Bitter cold
numbed fingers, crept in lungs and ached—well, maybe just
a little fire—a chance to open mail, to read
the words of love from home, they knew could be their last.

They knew the distant sound they heard; incredulous—
they stopped and listened: "*Stille Nacht, Heilige Nacht…*"
echoed across the dark, bounced off the ice and frost.
They answered—"*all is calm, all is bright…*"
Singing with strangers—enemies—impossible—
a concertina, a harmonica, guitar—
the cardboard sign: "NO FIGHT" where did the others find
the paint? White handkerchief, a soccer ball—
kicking, rolling, and laughter in the dark and mud;
a feast—Black Forest cake, biscuits and macaroons,
tobacco, coffee—shared and passed from hand to hand;
Commands ignored; shots fired, but only at the stars—
a memory only few would live to keep.

"The sun," he says, "would bring the battle. Christmas Day
erased the peace and good will. All the boys were men,
killing and being killed, not understanding why."
He hesitates, and gazes at the visitors
whose grandfathers had told this story years ago:
"Nobody knows the score—who won the soccer game.
But everyone recalls, after a century
the Carol—*Schlaf in himmlischer Ruh
Sleep in heavenly peace.*"

Little Thanksgivings

Give thanks to God, this day, for little things:
bee, dancing on a globe of clover;
sip of cold water,
smile from a stranger, a friend, a baby;
the alphabet, icicles, butter.

Be grateful to recover a lost trinket, to find
perfume of pine
or of summer rain, in morning's breath;
squeeze of a hand that reassures
in sad moments;
sunlight: glowing in a jar of jelly,
or pewter sheen on weathered wood.

Appreciate the rarely noticed:
a pillow's comfort;
wren that sings your name;
crow swirling the sky;
fingernails, teeth, eyelashes;
pencils, spoons, shoes; surprise of cinnamon,
violets that decorate the lawn.

Praise God for jokes, for minutes
of blessings that dash like chipmunks
across the surface of days,
jewels set in the frame
of memory.

Still horses graze on brown, snow-dusted hills
below eternal pines, infinite sky;
a river, born in ageless caverns, spills
down rocks of time to seas that never dry.
Red mountains, crowned with eagles, stand like kings
or priests, guarding a desert's mysteries.
A lark, a nightingale, a sparrow, sings
the same song through uncounted centuries.
Children in rubble, sunlight in tear-prisms,
flowers on graves, new mosses from charred earth
have more to say of God than catechisms.
Mourning is morning; death gives way for birth.
Life welds a chain no rust nor sword will sever;
only destruction cannot last forever.

Laura J. Bobrow

The Girl Who Could Not Decide

Samantha was proud of a copious cloud of
excessively lengthy, luxuriant hair.
At night when she brushed it, she smiled and she blushed. It
was something of which she took diligent care.

Each Sunday, shampoo day, she'd try out a new way
of styling her hair for the rest of the week.
First she washed, then she rinsed it till she was convinced it
was clean when it gave off that elegant squeak.

She made curls pinned with wire and sat under the dryer
to set a new style she had not tried before.
And beside her was ready (the thought made her heady)
a rose made of silk from the five-and-dime store.

It was meant to give flair to her stunning new hairdo,
the *pièce de résistance,* the finishing touch.
But when she first tried it, she could not decide. It
was not what she'd planned. She did not like it much.

She placed it up higher, took a glass to admire
the effect. No not there. It was certainly wrong.
On the side? Not there, either. Behind one ear? Neither.
Her arms soon grew tired. It was taking so long!

For hour after hour she toyed with that flower.
She was bound and determined to set it just so.
Her skin became paler, her eyes seemed to fail her.
Samantha was stubborn and would not let go.

Next morning they found her, a towel around her,
the flower in her left hand, the glass in her right.
A pretty disaster in pure alabaster,
Samantha had turned into stone overnight.

They moved her like that to the lawn as a statue.
The birds fluttered round her. They liked her a lot.
And one little wren did a thing which was splendid:
she fashioned her nest at the very best spot.

THE UNFORTUNATE BEETLE

A beetle and a queen, it's said,
were lovers in the royal bed.
(Believe it. In a fairy tale
such misalliances prevail.)

The king, in lieu of reprimands,
took justice in his royal hands.
He did not blame the beetle. No.
It was the queen who had to go.

He put some poison in a cup
and said to her, *Now, drink this up.*
Fine wine, my dear, to seal our vows,
as potent as the law allows.

Oh, thanks, she said. *A tiny sip.*
She raised the cup up to her lip.
Before she could allay her thirst
the beetle dived into it first.

My love, he cried, *it's not too late.*
I join you in your tragic fate!
He drank a bit. He swam around.
He hiccupped once, and then he drowned.

The queen sighed, *Darling bug, farewell.*
And from her eye one teardrop fell,
but she, be-jeweled and be-furred,
when prodded, gracefully demurred.

Woefully we must conclude
the beetle showed ineptitude.
He should have stopped to think it through.
It was a harebrained thing to do.

With other bugs the queen was smitten,
but of this beetle no more's written.
Their love was daft, the beetle dafter
to dream of happily ever after.

DEAR GOD, YOU MADE ME TOO SHORT.

LOVE, EVE.

Had I been given half a cubit more,
I would have seen our home and found it good.
I would have learned what I'd not known before:
we'd never find a better neighborhood.

If I'd have looked outside the garden wall,
if I had just been given ample height,
no tempter could ensnare me with his call.
I simply would have shut my ears up tight.

I would have stroked the robin in its nest.
I would have kissed the fishes in the pond.
I would have said to Adam, *Let us rest.*
No need to seek for what may lie beyond.

I would have snatched the serpent from the tree
and thrown him out to slither in the dust
while Adam brewed a pot of pekoe tea
and spoke to me of love instead of lust.

Jim Boucher

... And Some Are Posted Back Home

There's pain in black stone,
    That endures longer than the grimmest night;
    There's safety in black stone,
        That dresses torn flesh, and momentary fright.
        There's welcome in stone wedge,
            That extends its bent edges in sublime salute;
            There's dignity in stone wedge,
                That strikes its roll call in 58,000 names mute.
                There's recollection in wedge walk;
                    That contains records of families and friends.
                    There's healing in wedge walk,
                        That tempers the memories of tragic ends.
                There's sorrow in walk prayer,
                    That grieves over each death-bound mission;
                There's fidelity in walk prayer,
                    That recognizes their commitment to our nation.
                There's pride in prayer ritual,
                    That recalls the courage of heroes bound for glory;
                There's compassion in prayer ritual,
                    That recounts sad endings of each story.
            There's mystery in ritual cleansing,
                That springs from shadows clinging to heartbreak;
            There's grace in ritual cleansing,
            That seasons the taste of heartache.
        There's unity in cleansing black,
        That encodes the loneliness of all, fully as any one;
    There's love in cleansing black,
That preserves their honor in review for everyone.

Jack Callan

Rock Tree Boy
For N. Scott Momaday, author of *House Made of Dawn*

If it's magic, you start writing
while earth holds itself,
where bare is landscape
and takes me high above.
Don't be afraid, you never land,
clap your hands
and walk into the sunset.
If the bottom holds,
you can forget and go on
without the greasy handshake
of some Presidential man
who steals the fat
and camps on your land.

You are the gift that is given.

And I hear the buffalo in the sweetgrass
an' clench my sass.
Today, the day to find my way
among the great stars of universe,
just outta reach,
but on the way to Rainy Mountain.

I yearn to be home,
to hold foundation to teepee stake,
to top the world in blood memory,
to hold within our stories,
our need for rain,
and listening for medicine—
a god looking for his people—
the moon to exist
and be free,
imagination and the farther world,
that moon in two windows—not taken by surprise,
and I, in trouble,
write in that moment, tear paper,
and cry.

Sojourn in Gilead

I was hauled to the woodshed
by the angel of Silence—
slammed to the ground, then tied to a chair.
She didn't read me my rights in the barkin' of sin.
Kept a snarlin' pitbull who wouldn't stop flashin' his badge,
hurlin' insults,
interruptin' my testimony—
"Your Honor?" I said, where none was found. Got nowhere.
The heart of the matter
was never attained,
just a field of flame and featherings.
We rolled in sacred dust and splinters,
both armed with truth, called democracy.
She called for my surrender and began to tire.
I liked my chances
in the two-against-one. I waited patiently.
When, quick on my feet
and dodgin' their blows,
I undid my bindings—sat straight in the chair.
Lookin' them in the eye, I could see right into 'em.
(They didn't like that.)
Her surly bulldog was losin' his grip,
kept tryin' to bite me from behind.
I said, "Sit," and his tail tucked.
(No real fight in this dog.)
Still two-to-one and holdin' my own,
I asked, "What was your point?"
"Repentance!" she cried.
"You got the wrong man," I replied, and left it at that.
(She called for prayer.)
Who knows what was said?
The bulldog just sat there, a sweatin'.
Ol' Jacob limped…but I got away.

Joan Ellen Casey

Vacation

Trunks of red maple and scrub pine
covered with lichen like green glitter
stand in black water.

Purple pickerel bend beneath
the weight of birds with short song.
Silence calls the wild horses.

I hold pain in my hand
then let it drop from my fingers
off the pier into Currituck Sound.

On the sea side of the outer bank,
waves crash ashore with the sound
of wind captured from the last hurricane.

Dark pushes the sun out of the sky,
and crabbers with flashlights flood
the beach like fireflies.

Moonlight melts cloud
and turns on the stars
in your eyes.

A bit of eternity
is caught in time.

Journeying

In fragile bodies
alone in our space of time
we ride together.

The Squirrel Who Answered the Bird

It was a cold Covid morn
that had swept the streets
of the living except for
two dogs that barked
at the wind and the one bird
that sang and was answered
by a squirrel.

I felt sense deprived.
My peace was shattered
by the stillness that stopped
everything around me
until the images in my mind
were fashioned by what I saw
and heard on YouTube the night before:

a hawk walking back and forth on a see-saw
a puppy trying to play with a statue
a deer jumping waves at the beach
the shadow of a ballerina
dancing across the walls of a courtyard
pirouetting en pointe at the top of a dome
to the music of "Spoon River."

When I let Van Gogh's starry night
and field of sunflowers into the
darkness of my soul, I understood
how he suffered for his sanity
seeing flaming clouds, rainbows
in someone's skin, and how
green glowed in water.

The videos filled up my senses.
I wanted to capture such beauty—
so real and intense—that made me feel
like flying off a cliff.
But like the squirrel, I am finding it hard
to sing that lovely song.

Kenneth F. Conklin

Darling of Darkness

Darling of darkness
Where are you now
I've danced on dark clouds
I've played on the bow
I've tried new roads
And looked at the old
Marched up and down alleys
Stood out in the cold
Lived by the clock
With no sense of time
Spent a lot on nothing
With my last dime
Told people about me
Without listening to them
Fallen deeply in love
And back out again
Fallen deeper still
Didn't like the trash
Learned not to kill
But paid in cash
Been up to the top
To see what was there
Saw nothing I wanted
But stood there to stare
Now I am floating
In space without air
Hoping to find
Someone to share
All the dreams of my mind
And thoughts of despair
But mostly I need
Someone who cares

They Don't Make Forever Like They Used To

At the One-Half Lounge
Crooning 'Sail Away'
Or, 'Georgia on My Mind'
Or, 'Pour Me Another Vacation'

Sometimes meeting me at Muddy Waters
Drinking coffee, lamenting about the times
Paranoia setting in
Pettiness robbing your genius

You finally let go of the drugs
And the alcohol
Never the women, though
And certainly never the artistry

And such songs they were
With Hendrix and Webb
With some Sinatra sprinkled in
To keep us grounded

And at the Iridium
When Les Paul himself invited you on stage
You brought the house down
As you knew you would

In the key of 'Wichita Lineman'
You painted a picture for me
An oriental 'Irisis'
And to this day it is there

And the time you cried
Letting your Bukowski shield down
Your uncloaked heart showing
Your brilliance, misunderstood

You would hate
That YouTube has you now
But you welcomed the band of angels
Saying, Sheldon
We are coming to carry you home
We are coming to carry you home

Leaving Fourth Street

I will leave behind my gardening tools
And the special shelves
I built for the kitchen pantry
The ocean continues to pound
As it always has while
The seagulls circle and screech
I will never open this front door again
To my home at the beach

The bamboo branches are mourning
While the moving van is loaded
With all my stuff, eastward bound
Its diesel engine idling
I wave goodbye to neighbors
(Come see us soon)
I will never open this front door again
To my home at the beach

While my favorite chair is finally loaded
As is the 'To Beach' sign pointing west
Be well old eucalyptus friend
Be at one with the salt-laced breeze
Why won't someone convince me to stay!
Or reinstate the job I lost
I will never leave for just the day again
And return to my home at the beach

TERRY COX-JOSEPH

EXCHANGE STUDENT

I

She was just a teenager. How was I to know?
If I could go back and do it all again

I would give her a hug, take her to a movie
make more rules, more conversation

give her more chores, more salsa,
more parties and never
leave her
alone.

II

She was fourteen.
Why did I think she was different?

Third World country,
no screens on her windows,

power just three hours a day,
government bankrupt, postal workers gone,

thugs so poor they used broken glass
instead of guns. Everyone left for Canada.

Einstein could have told us that poverty never equals the mass
of homesickness squared. Who cared

about braces and new shoes? She craved routine, jalapeños and
curried rice, tradition and ritual,

embraced, instead, friends who skipped school,
stole liquor. In the end, she couldn't care less

about anything except insisting that she hated me,
like a fourteen-year-old in any country.

Cause for Concern

Newscasters pan bloated
bodies floating.
New Orleans floodwaters—
some people stayed.
No cars, didn't even walk.
Why?

Here, feather-haired drunk
urinates on sidewalk,
plate glass window.
Art patrons stare. Can't get
his zipper up, fingers tremble,
eyes pink as paint.

He could have been
one of those.
One who stayed,
his only option another swig,
their only option help
that couldn't come—
Big Brother would protect,
always be there.

They couldn't grasp the enormity
just as I didn't understand
why some stayed behind.

He doesn't see me,
creases between my brows,
palm pressed against agitated
stomach. Won't know
that I squeeze my phone, debate
whether to call police,
buy him a sandwich,
walk away

He will never wonder,
why?

Coffee House Reprise

Awnings shade café tables, hint
of Paris, *amour, ah, oui,* couples
sip espresso, dogs cozy up for a nap.

Freshly ground java, seductive caress
of Cary Grant and Grace Kelly,
hand-on-hip taunt of Lena Horne.

Scuffed wood floor like you've walked
into your own kitchen, worn tabletops
and chatter, cherry pastries behind glass.

You long to swallow forkfuls of comfort,
tip back a poem. Feed your soul
words that sparkle like champagne.

Kathleen P. Decker

Trees in Snow

simple phrase
trees in snow
look closer

spiky oak branches
dull-brown, covered with thin linear deposits
luxurious head of hair, highlighted with age

tufts of white settled in niches
of dwarf arborvitae, powder puffs on its tips
shouts *Christmas*, even after

fire-red branches of dogwood
tint pink the snow covering them
contrast with arborvitae, echoing *Noel*

contorted filbert, catkins veiled in white
the snow-load on its corkscrew branches and stems
forms an icy Afro

all this white
colored persimmon as the sun sets
blue sky streaked with red
between gaps in the tree line
fades to grey so quickly

during the mid-winter days
earth beneath its ivory cloak
hides its buds and bugs
waiting, waiting…

perched on a fence post
flitting to a tree
a pair of cardinals
his scarlet, her dull russet plumage
flash bright against cream
they know
spring is coming

MONARCHS

most prevalent
of butterflies
All-American, north and central
so regal and strong, its coloration
imitated by lesser butterflies
painted ladies, peacocks,
viceroys and queens

throngs of migrating monarchs
cover acres of Mexican jungle
with gold, rust, and black flutters
in winter…
endangered
milkweed replaced
with urban condos
winter with warming

I dream of
planting milkweed
among butterfly bushes
sowing milkweed
in county parks, meadows
and the yards of urban condos
so monarchs reign again

Pamela Brothers Denyes

What to Carry with You
For my grandchildren

No *thing* can go with you.
Carry the brightest thoughts,
irreplaceable loving feelings,
bright hope for the future
and the joyful sweetness
that is your youth.

Give away the rest, spend
yourself and those worldly
goods on the people you love,
and share some with those
who have little to build
a life on at all.

Let loving kindness be your honest
life's work. Every big decision
is a choice between love and fear,
for they resolve always to these.
Choose love and it will be the spark
for success lifting all your days.

Use your one life's energy for good,
for progress without pretension,
holding to love's instructions,
which you will always hear
if you keep your truest self
alive inside and out.

Mrs. Creekmore's May Peas

Stormed hard this morning
after that tragedy yesterday where
anger boiled and two guns killed
twelve, a first in my hometown.

Not sure Mrs. Creekmore had the
May peas I wanted, but she did. I know
when I go there that she will sell me
whatever's going to be on my stove tonight.

Mrs. Creekmore and I didn't speak of it,
the nearby slaughter, only pretty peas, red
potatoes for my pot, and strong young
onions, thinned from her garden.

Home from the farmer's market,
I shelled peas in silence and in pain.
Shelling peas gives you time,
time enough to think about yesterday.

Sweet May peas fell from my fingers
as I released them from sturdy pods,
gently freeing them, so as not to bruise
nor break nor bleed nor kill.

What unspoken ugly pain wracked this
killer of twelve co-workers?
Why did no one notice his anger,
so crazy it erupted in unholy murder?

Surely this sick man's murderous spree was
not about work, but about fear and anger.
Can't we be mindful of each other's pain
and choose to ask the hard questions?

I went to Mrs. Creekmore's again today.
She had Mama and all her sisters there, and
somebody's husband, all together, keeping
each other close, like peas safe in a pod.

Honest as Open Wind

Naked and free,
honest as open wind
visibly rippling miles
of supple prairie grasses,
stripped to purest snow,
white like a tiny seed,
a blossom fallen to the
solid warm soil beneath,

simple as the first
words you remember
from your child's mind,
I will speak from there.

What will you hear?

SHARON CANFIELD DORSEY

DAUGHTER OF THE MOUNTAINS

Growing up in the mountains of Appalachia,
it really snowed,
glazing the circling peaks with sparkling white powder
that made children pray for a day off from school,
and mothers cast their grateful eyes skyward
when the yellow bus showed up anyway.

Snowy mornings still conjure images of my dad
carrying buckets of coal to fire up the big iron cooking
stove. The aroma of sizzling bacon and hot biscuits
evokes the chill of icy linoleum under my feet
as I dashed from beneath a mound of warm quilts
to shiver beside the roaring stove.

When the mountains gave up their icy crown in spring,
crystal water gurgled down the steep slopes to settle in
rocky creeks, home to bass that would grace our table,
served with cornbread and ramps—the wild onions
we dug from the deepest, darkest places in the woods, their
secret location passed down, grandfather to father to son.

My dad and his brothers were indentured to coal,
black gold they dug from the bowels of the mountain.
When the wailing sirens signaled a cave-in,
families huddled at the mouth of the mine,
waiting to see who the angry mountain had claimed.
The mountains gave and the mountains took away.

At twenty, I packed up my few possessions
and my brand-new husband,
and I left the mountains, forever, I thought,
only to learn as years went by,
the mountains never really left me.
Like demanding parents, they continue to call me back.

Summer Leaves the Hills

Summer *ripens* into fall in the hills.

The last of the garden harvest is done.
Cellars overflow with bulging burlap bags of
potatoes, apples, nuts; rainbow-hued jars filled
with vegetables and fruits line wooden shelves.

Air grows crisp and pungent with the scent
of burning leaves; southbound geese cry goodbye.
The scarlet crown of autumn signals briefer days,
longer, cooler nights under eider down quilts.

Pale sun scatters frosted light on bare ground,
where lately yellow poppies spread gold filigree
on the hillsides. Green time is gone.
Wild roses and fragrant sage are dead.

Frost nips the dawn.
Forest beasts seek homes,
their heartbeats still.
Human beasts rest

as autumn *marches* across the summer hills.

Love Is a Perfect Pineapple

A glance in my rear-view mirror
reveals an unfolding family tableau.
Feeling a little guilty but curious,
I sit transfixed, unobtrusive, watching.

Two people lift an elderly man into a wheelchair.
The woman covers his gaunt frame with a plaid blanket.
A young man adjusts a white mask over his nose, mouth.
I wonder…wife, son?

They trundle him into the grocery store.
I follow, my own list in hand.
We separate at the door, but cross
paths again later as I wait at the check-out.

The wheelchair shopper is surveying pineapples.
He picks up one, turns it, sniffs, and puts it back.
Again—choose, scrutinize, sniff, reject.
For once, I'm glad my check-out line is slow.

After four rejections, he nods his head,
places the chosen fruit into the basket.
I catch a glimpse of twinkling eyes and
know he is smiling behind the white mask.

Over his head, the woman and man exchange smiles.
I feel tears welling in the back of my throat.
Happiness today is the search for a perfect pineapple.
Love is allowing the adventure to happen.

Linda Ankrah-Dove

Synaptic World View

Despite all the news and the stress, despite everything,
do you too want to stay serene and safe?

The wisdom pundits advise daily gratitudes
to reduce blood pressure. I've been doing that.

On waking (instead of listing what I must get done today)
I think of four things and give thanks—

my good dog, my good health, my good friend,
my tart green rhubarb showing off its swirling skirts.

I've done this gratitude thing for a year or two now
and it works to some extent—because, they say,

synapses in our plastic brains connect and reconnect
to map our world for us.

But, lately, how my brain frames my world is not my focus.
It's my heart in pain yearning for unworldly miracles.

Across the night sky I hear the Milky Way composing
eulogies for mankind as we take giant leaps into past time,

failing to hear the stars lamenting our earth mother
whose dimming orb we disregard

and failing in our time to imagine an alternative response
to prevent her asthmatic suffocation.

GRAVITATIONAL PULL

A pile of pleated, no-iron skirts
green, pink, and polyester purple.
White shirts, collars stiff and starched,
She thrusts her arms deep in, a dolphin
churning colors into ocean storms
on a swelling tide, needing food,
intent on the search.

The old oak chest creaks its joints.
Through mothball-mush her hands stroke
disintegrating woolen knits,
their feel like flailing seaweed fronds
as deeper to the wooden seabed
she dives, her body quivering, intent
on her essential quest.

Waves of doubt sweep her back and forth.
The father who walked away one day,
mother at the stove, the hearth, the sink,
submerged by penny-pinching,
drowned in a lifetime of making do,
too worn out to notice love's potential,
dead at forty-two.

Her fingers fumble a small, globed object,
a pebble perhaps, filed smooth by years.
But in the underwater the low glow
suggests something metal to her palm.
Her right hand grasps it tight, draws it up
through the churnings, and holds it high
towards revealing light.

A silver locket, its brittle clasp breaking.
It opens, fragile as a sea shell. But
there's no echo in her listening ear,
no lock of wavy greying hair, no beloved face
in a faded photo, no inked message
as in a drifted, blue-oceaned bottle
borne in on the rising tide that now recedes.

Dinggedicht

Things of this world speak for themselves.
I am merely a scrivener, an imperfect scrivener.
I strive to record things just as they are
but my human perception gets in the way.
I try to describe in accurate detail
everyday objects—a kitchen tray,
a discarded pail in the yard.
But I catch myself likening the gleam
of a crocus as it dances the wind
to a flashlight's beam scudding the night.
I pronounce rushing waters in flood
as furious, angry, raging. The groan of a storm
as forlorn Prometheus oppressed by the world.
But the slurred warble of finches, the wren's chatter,
the woodpecker's hammer—their voices
speak for themselves, not through my pen.
I pray though that I am not merely a mockingbird,
who transcribes the form of things
but is blind and deaf to things alive in themselves.

I Recall between Moons

the way of the hawk the rabbit the shadows.
Land bleeding into our clothes.
Pokeberry. Walnut husks. Dandelions—
for whimsy, for tea, for tincture, for nine shades of yellow: root to ray floret.
A time my leftblood lineage lived for field and sheep. For laughter.
Pitchforks raised in joy, in sustenance, not labor.

My people stole this from my people
then offered whiteness.
We cowardly accept and accept and accept.

Where might this shade of erasure
go from here. The dust of my bones has forgotten.
They are heavy. Our centuries.

We whittle lungnotes.
Command allegiance.
No, hypnotize. No,
forgetting. Inherit
from my father's mother's father's mother. Whom i love
as i love my father and my father's mother.

When roots exhausted of their own reaching
turn dormant when autumn sumacs' songs of saffron
sing disquiets into winter's sleep. Take no shortcut
to our gathering place in the wildness. Name us
at our widening.

Name my skin jaundiced. Name us butter. Name us splotched
as unripened berries. Name us breeze and ocean and salt.
And light through whiskey. Name us grapevine bent and woven.
Harm torn from peach trees made into useful things like baskets and fishtraps.

We must be more than—

Thistle: Myth or Medicine?

Cones pulse fat with Mary's milk
because this mother knows
we are always afraid
of not having enough.

Tonic to the liver. Liver—
organ of anger. Anger
yellow shroud of fear
dwells in our bladders.

Turns us to stone.

Rise and Fall of the Republic

Spotted Touch-Me-Not
Each flower hangs
as an opulent orange mouth
tangerine tongue lip-draped
red spots ride the lick

As husks mature
the lightest touch expels their seeds

Dehiscence—the splitting or
bursting open of a bur or wound

Sometimes the lightest touch is love
Sometimes armor must split open

John L. Dutton II

Walking My Human

Each day, I walk my human.
I love watching his mood change
the farther we get from home.
I know he's not
the sharpest tool in the shed,
as he often forgets my name.
He calls me Ucker, or
he confuses me with a duck, of all things.
I am NOT a ducking dog.
What a fool he is!
I'll sniff and point
and eat so much juicy grass tips,
that he thinks I'm a cow.
I'll wander aimlessly and
take him on these
monstrously
long
walks.
My god, he needs it.
He's got a spare tire with him,
and we're not even driving!
He's fat,
and I am not talking PH phat.
I love when we are an hour or so
into the walk,
and he gets the zombie eyes.
I'll wait for one of my friends to come out,
Sammy Squirrel or Robby Robin,
and then I'll bolt.
Man, I can sometimes hear his shoulder
pop out
of his socket!
I haven't knocked him over yet,
but you can't say I'm not trying.
My human pampers me.
He cleans up my poo,
sometimes getting it on his hands or shoe.
He'll chauffeur me around town
to some of my favorite designer stores,
Petco or Off the Leash.
He drops a bundle of cash at these stores
just for me.

You'll die for those mani-pedis at the salon.
They're not cheap,
but I'm worth every penny.
Everyone stops to compliment me,
and not once have I heard anyone tell me
"Hey, that's a good-looking human you have there."
If you haven't gotten yourself a human yet,
you're missing out!
I'd go get one today,
and let your entitlement begin.
See you later,
when I am out
walking my human.

HOME

As I lie exhausted on the couch,
I dwell in slovenly comfort
During the final hours
Of another satisfyingly
Frustrating day.
I know not every task was completed,
Yet something was checked off
The never-ending
"To-Do" list of life.
I find comfort around me
And think,
"Home is where the heart is."
Clothes strewn on the floor.
Books piled in every nook.
Dog curled on my lap.
TV murmurs in the background.
Kids stomping the stairs.
Dishes stacked precariously.
Mismatched socks seeking lonely shoes.
Toys in every corner.
Wife reading in her favorite chair.
My coffee cup in hand.
I exhale and let the day fall from my shoulders.
I have found comfort in the clutter.

Gᴏᴅ's Cᴀᴛʜᴇᴅʀᴀʟ
    Written in Thunder Hole, Acadia National Park, Maine,
    as I watch the kids rock climbing, 7.20.2018

God's Cathedral was not made by man's hand;
It was made by the wind, the sea, the sand, and the soil.
There is no timetable or tools required to build this house of worship,
The only item required to raise this holy house is time;
Time's toolbox cannot be contained!
Thunder, lightning, wind, rain, surf, sand, snow, and hail—
Tools that toil the earth constantly crafting its beauty.
No one who worships here wears their Sunday best or waits for the Sabbath.
No offering is collected—
The only tribute paid is the sweat running down one's back
and the solace one finds in contemplation after challenging oneself to venture
    outside.
The choir consists of waves breaking upon the shore.
The creatures chirp and chatter the sermon endlessly.
The breeze rejuvenates the congregation
who, when ready, rise to continue onward deeper into the forest.

Anne Emerson

Chambers of the Heart

A coiling many-chambered human heart—
a nautilus—in death it breaks apart;
its form deforming under stilling sand,
unless recaptured by a human hand.

By pearl and silk, or dirt and rags rebuilt,
a shell grants someone brilliance or guilt.
So, was he soaring to creative life;
or shellfish, butchered by convention's knife?

That person whom we loved—a man or saint?
The one derided—villain? Oddly quaint?
What author walks the beach to pick it up—
our spiral shell—and see its heart lit up?

Its owner breathed and moved in sandy bed;
we might have known him there; not raised him, dead.
Let's make him once-more living—give him style—
avoiding hasty judgment without trial.

How lies the light upon the sand today?
Who walks with us, about the salted bay?
Alas, a different shell entices on,
while waves envelop this; its moment gone.

L. Nelson Farley

Seeing You

I see in your eyes
The gleam of youth
Radiating enthusiasm
Radiating anticipation
As in a first love.

I see in you
Wisdom and tact
The reward of learning
From many years.

I see in you
The love and trust
Of a newborn
Recently entrusted to mankind
By nurturing angels.

I see in you a curiosity
Of a toddler, not yet
Able to discern the
Danger of Drano;
As discernment developed
Your curiosity remained, unabated.

I see in you
The zest for life
Of a child: playfulness.
And of an adult:
Focusing effort on a specific goal.
Meaning has been added to playfulness.

I see in you
The achieving of one in their prime
Molding words into poems,
And sound into music
Achievement has been added to meaning.

Life is after all
A sum of all its ages.
I see in you
The sum of them all;
A coordination of them all.

Maurice Ferguson

Conquistador

As a young hombre he pursued escapades
beyond these distant mountain passes.
Now summits and adventures
neither beckon nor summon him
as no surprise or marvel kindles his heart.
Chivalry died long before he was born.

When young, brave deeds he dreamed,
themes Spain's troubadours sang
while they traveled through his Andalusia
of men compelled to bear arms
in defense of noble worthiness
against the infidels at Alhambra's gates.

Now, neither gold ingot nor silver bullion
please the conquistador. A shadow has fallen
across his scarred and battered visor
while he kneels like twilight kneels
to his evening vespers. It appears
the picturesque has become the mere picayune.

Perhaps, he grieves for a much simpler time
when vintner and vintage were entwined
as neighbor with neighbors stomped
their vintage grapes and raised their flagons
and flasks to Bacchus—ah, to hear him
sing such amorous serenades.

Or, maybe, old age and second thoughts,
such as the recollection of how he set
his almonds and olives in straight orderly rows
or the time he rode his frisky stallion
to the sepulcher of St. James where vigilers
spun yarns beneath night's brilliant stars
while all the señoritas shook their castanets
round the dancing campfire flames.

Oh, my weary conquistador, your querulous eyes
hang in the master's painting like
some dangling participle.
Your enigmatic teardrop smears
a question mark upon the canvas

for us to squint at to decipher.
Always, the explanations hide in a foreign
landscape beyond the boundaries of
the master's frame, buried in a land
beyond the setting sun, on horizons beyond the sea
yet some il Pensimoso beneath the surface
tugs and yanks for answers.

Tell me, did the unscrupulous el capitán
gloat over the stones of Tenochtitlan
when the temple gods were toppled?
Did you wince and look the other way
when the gutted Sun King crawled
from his extravagant throne?

Did you flinch when no sacred
Quetzalcoatl divinely intervened
to spare the plumed emperor?
Did you condone all those who
hurriedly Christianized the maidens
for slavery and intercourse?

Who can ever decide what is truth?
Your tarnished eyes speak volumes
as if Velásquez abandoned you
between sea cliff and oncoming tide—
the last knight amid a vanguard
of cut-throat mercenaries.

Catherine Fletcher

Heat Run

head up water surge the great lady blows
hump back emerges awash in vapor
she arches slips back down below
undulating close to the surface
tail swishing she turns reveals her white belly pleats
as flippers scull and stroke water
again she rolls underneath as grey observers
intensely consider

she's off!
running in heat

one and two and then there's seven
in hot pursuit!
forty-ton suitors charge at high speed jostle position
slap smack the surface submerge
baritones roar bubbles
chasing her tail

she:
leads them on through the juice teasing increasing the pace

they:
jump flippers lashing thrashing peduncles rivals collide
with intent to kill

one's got a bleeding rostrum
another torn fins
boys bellow and force each other downward
the brine resounds with almighty battling
competitors vanish into turbulent froth

mr. black breaches leeward
swerves thrusts forward

breaks from the brawl and
she's caught!
burbling near the water line
ripples mingle eddies dissolve
as she and he sail beside one another
triumphant two giant humped backs slip
under creamy white wakes under crests and troughs

stroking rubbing merging
they freedive
penetrating the depths
singing the ocean's immeasurable
pleasurable song

Song of the Cynic
After Federico García Lorca

Life after life passes as the earth simply spins.
Trees sleep.
No prayers bring the moon closer.
The air's thick with sweetness
but a tiger sits in my throat.
I follow my own footsteps and wonder,
Where, where does the light go?

I want to drip with July rains.
I want to merge with crashing seas.
I want to feel the planet's hum,
witness the fires of polar skies—colors of God whispering—
run with wild horses on the isle of Assateague.

Shall I turn another corner?
Mourn for days that eyes can no longer see?
Tell me, Heart, is it from deep bitterness
that faith is conceived?

RICH FOLLETT

DIDELPHIS VIRGINIANA

just before bedtime,
barefoot and nightshirted,
cursing an early frost,
i was tipping kitchen trash into
a bin outside the house
when something inside the bin … *moved.*

time stood still
(no other way to say it)
and 'zero at the bone'
became real.

survival instinct
put a nearby spade in my hand;
blind panic
drove me to wield it like a shackled convict
digging post holes in blood-red clay
at the height of a southern summer
under the foreman's rifled gaze.

my victim was silent
(i could have weathered anything but *that*):
to this day, the briefest stagnation of night air
reanimates that voiceless black and
it is *i* who cannot scream …

i did not—
could not—
revisit the scene
until daylight
breached my chrysalis of terror.

gingerly peeling back detritus,
i peered into the vinyl abyss
expecting to find, perhaps,
fragments of furry hide or,
at the very least,
a deflated rodent balloon;

i was not prepared for
the infant opossum
which seemed merely to be asleep until
i noticed the gaping crimson crescent
where its right side should have been.

for the record,
i have never liked opossum
(ever since child—i startled one
while climbing a hollow tree and
it hissed me into
acrid saffron self-saturation).

many times since
i have allowed my car to drift toward
a headlight-dazed midnight marsupial,
secretly coveting the satisfying *crunch*
i knew would follow—
of this i am not proud, but
the facts remain.

having been born between wars—
too young for one, too old for another—
i had no referent for
myself as assassin;
this infant rind of mangled fur
had broken, in death,
my steely resolve—
my seething animosity.

compassion and guilt
flooded me,
hollowed me,
and so it is that
twenty years on
i dream the spade untouched—
the creature, whole....

PEEPER PAEAN

in precisely the same way the sun appears
(an apricot promise
of glorious streams over crested blue ridgeline) —

in just that heady way,
the peepers are singing:
their raucous tintinnabulation
an invitation to ribald chaos.

the renaissance in all its glory
held nothing o'er this Lilliputian jostle and thrum;
all creation echoes their chiming desire
to multiply.

ephemeral and fey,
piping their pleasure to passersby,
these minute amphibian minstrels
ignite dormant fancies,
erasing the ravage of time;
rejuvenating all who savor
their ardent call.

is it any wonder that
grizzled workmen and
wizened crones
will pause their withering grind
at the first strain of
giddy peeper roundelay?

ponce de leon
(had he known of their occamy)
would have drunk deeply
the silvered essence of their jubilant refrain.

here in the pungent womb of springy night
i thrill to their cacophonous air;
holding my breath,
willing my plenary being to
absorb their aural essence—

savoring each harmonic morsel,
gathering seeds of transcendent joy
to be recalled in friendless days of
silent-seeming winter.

in precisely the same way the stars ascend
(a shimmering garland
of lustrous dreams over moonlit silk horizon)—

in just that glimmering way,
the peepers are singing:
their riotous discombobulation
an exhortation—

abandon pathos.

Eric J. Forsbergh

Lobstering at 96

The greasy swells are out today. Tides tie my schedule,
half-adrift upon her death last year.

My skin sprouts barnacles and mats of kelp. So thin
it tears against a tightened line. Bruises spread

like algae blooms in blue. Whips of salt spume toughen
even skinny boys. She married to unpeel me the man. Today,

I combed her plot with care. What with the cemetery poorly kept,
my friends might well be buried in a vacant lot. My neighbors are

their sprat. They strut like gulls, innocent of history.
Not the blizzard of '50 when every boat and car

was clamped in ice three weeks, the sea a sullen gray,
and half the fishing shacks were pick-up sticks.

The warmer weather is a weakling nowadays. Between
sinews and my knobby joints, these limbs resemble

knotted rope. Still, I had to haul the pots. The sea, and she,
are all I care to know. I learned eddies from flow,

surface from undertow. My jury is the clouds, the sun,
the wind. Lobsters molt. July's their naked month, but

I'll not be reborn. With her, one long visit to the county fair
was plentiful. And she won't meet me at the gate again.

I'll be grateful when I shed my shell this once.

On a Surgeon Poet

A wound on paper isn't quite a wound.
It's a distant diagnosis, lying on clean sheets,
no seeps or stains, untreatable, a page unanswered

while in the moment I confer with Mr. Abdi,
who shifts his weight to parry pain
when the nib becomes a knife.

They say reflection-action alternates:
A metronome seeks symmetry either way.
Some schools of medicine are introducing

verse, tempering the old vice-versa: the need to
operate or not. A new contemplation in a new
sequestered space. First, listen to the patient. Balance

every phrase, and how the pauses weigh. Follow
the mouth trying to translate for the eyes. Observe
the aging face plowed under by its grievances. All poetry.

Saturdays, in the belly of a bookstore, it's me and words.
When one darts me from an unexpected angle, I suck in my breath.
Already sitting, I shrink myself enough to slip inside a sorrow

fragile as a sparrow, or into a brittle tuft of radiated hair, or
someone else's final lover, or the skin's gray paste of kidney failure,
perhaps a whitewashed family, or an old Somali castigating death.

But by Sunday afternoon, my eyes begin to flit and skim
along a line that tries to lead me on: a track across
an endless field of snow. And I miss the imperative of blood.

Chapman Hood Frazier

Owlets

The spring my brother and I found the owlets in the ivy
was the time Mother left us with our grandmother

to meet her French lover. They had been abandoned
wobbling among the vines like little white dolls, downy

with white tufts of feathers. Their golden eyes unblinking
could swivel off their missing necks almost all the way around.

I caught them in Father's garden gloves then carried them
to the garage in a shoe box. My brother had made a nest

from a wooden crate he'd found there and filled with grass clippings,
pine straw and some flower petals to make it beautiful.

We caught them worms, a couple beetles and brought them carrots
from the refrigerator, and bread. We filled a plastic bowl with water.

The X of their feet were like little endings. We placed them beneath
the large hickory in the side yard and waited to see their mother

return but she never did. At night, we opened the top of the box
so she would see them. We knew she could see in the dark.

By morning, we found one standing on the other and in its beak
a downy feather. What was uneaten we buried in the backyard

near the lilac in a shoe box. By evening the second one died too.
We watched the hickory and the ivy but she never returned.

Bestiary

Each letter has an animal self, a dreamscape's sound surge
of scale and claw purged in a moment's bright breath
of hiss or thunder. Its flutter borne from umber and burnt

sienna, bone crush and manganese blown around a hand
on a rock face, just where the voice reverberates its
syllabic dance in a wrist flick and moan, urging forth the herd

or causing rain to cross the plain in a purpling bruise. This,

the opening in the monoglot of tongue, something to listen for
something to lock in, lift and remember. This is the faint blue

hued by light across an expectant eye, a crimson
whisper in a breath where each detail of nuthatch or katydid,
skink or smoke haze begins its slow fade towards extinction.

This is what's frayed here found among strung beads of jasper,
tourmaline, a Nassarius shell smudged in red ochre,
a final act spoken; a totem dreamed forth in cut amber

caught, microbe by microbe, in a silence becoming mind.

CROW

You're the philosopher of funk, reading salvation in opossum entrails
on the roadside with your cock-eyed musings and morning call.

Street smart, you see art in the fine stink of distinction as you two-step
traffic in an awkward hump and flap to continue your close reading

of carcass. The ultimate deconstructionist, you pick each text in your rite
of dismemberment, gorging on the relativity of the body and gray haze of

after thought, calling into question the word, "ruin." Oh, dark god
of afterlife, you sense in decay the apocrypha of salvation. Oh,

hawk chaser, defender of the decomposed, you never forget a face, in your wink
and nod, picking it eyeless like the relic it becomes. Each martyr bone

is for your séance of one chanted in your strange morphology of tongue.
Oh, confessor of the fetid, you caw from the *Book of Shadows* a myth

of resurrection into question, then in your boneyard dance of redemption,
you prick the locks of the body bare in your split-tongued spell.

For this is your baptism of stench. This, your holy rant for rain, death is
but a black catechism caught mid-croak rising in your throat,

the muttered reflux of forever. Or, is it just more dark sarcasm in your
blue-black stutter and limp, a final, eulogized, and godless joke?

Greg Friedmann

When Ponds Froze in Virginia

I try to tell the young man what it was like
when ponds froze in Virginia
and you could skate under stars
bright enough to see by. He shrugs:
Guess you can't miss what you never knew.
So here then, if you would know: there was a time
when ponds froze in Virginia. If the weather
stayed calm, they'd freeze like glass.
If the moon was full, you'd see leaves of
pond-bottom grasses below you as you flew.
If you were as light and as brave as a teenager,
you could ignore the creaking of the ice
as you sailed across it, far into a night
lit only by stars you could see by.
If you dared, you could skate away from
the others talking in clusters by the fire
and skate so far into the night that all you'd hear
was your breath, the wind on your ears,
your skates sliding on glass, and the low groans
of creaking ice you hoped wouldn't give.

The Lone Merganser

Mergansers come through in the last days of winter,
Making their way back north. Called 'common,'
They are grossly misnamed: the male, a striking contrast

Of white body, black back, and head of deeply luminous
Green; the female's frame a blended wash, her head a bright rust,
Topped with a bold crest that drapes behind and down her neck.

Their flock of a dozen dwindles as do the days of March,
Until only three remain up the channel: a drake and two females.
Each day as I walk in the warming weather I expect to find them gone;

Yet these three abide. One day they are gone; then no sign
For a week. Then she appears, floating close to the bank
As if for shelter: a lonely female—or only seeming lonely to me,

As I first knew her as one of three. She glides alone, dipping
Her head in the stream, then flipping it up and back, her ruddy crest
Throwing droplets that flash with sunshine as they fly.
Her beauty is hers alone, with no drake nearby.

Sue Davis Gabbay

At Hickory Hill, July 30, 1864

The cool spring water bubbles up
relief and refreshment
to all who come to kneel beside it.
The old tin cup rattles on its stake
echoing the not-so-distant cannon fire.
To the spring come the weary,
the wounded, the young boys away
from town or farm for the first time,
seeking a moment of respite.
Yankee Jack splashes his face and head,
drinks deep, turns to offer the cup
to Johnny Reb at his side.
Hands touch,
torn blue sleeve beside ragged gray.
They exchange brief glances
seeing each in the other the wound
deeper than bullet or sword can inflict,
a wound to the spirit, never to heal.
Bodily thirst quenched, the two
return to their separate camps, both
athirst for home.

James F. Gaines

Portrait of the Artist as a Fisherman Watching the Moon
Inspired by a woodblock by Hokusai

Hokusai, you must be modest, or more honest than some men
I draw myself bristling anachronistically with hair and brawn
Sitting on a granite boulder by a Massachusetts pond
Hawkeyed with untested ideals and unquenched ambition
Savoring a diaphanous, floating moon in August skies
But there you are, sensei, so ostensibly shoddy
Chimp-browed, pug-nosed, unkempt with stubbled jaws
Absurdly unheroic in your straw skirt and leather gaiters
Drawing on a tiny pipe like a Popeye gone to seed
And you haven't even bothered to unfurl your fishing line
From the pole of bamboo cane that rests idly by the creel
Damn! Once again you've tricked me, you master of litotes
This understatement is the height of your benign deceit

Ushibori in Hitachi Province
Inspired by a woodblock by Hokusai

Truly this is the real floating world
Putting the lie to the glitz of imperial Edo
And its flocks of prostitutes and hangers-on
Here in the tranquil everyday
A brace of herons rises above the reeds
As the boatman tips his bucket over the side
Adding borrowed water back into the marsh
Redundant but ever so profound
All shipshape now onboard
With gear neatly stowed he sighs
Sails artfully rolled rest beneath the boom
Another silent evening settles at Fuji's feet
Where ageless hamlets cluster in blue shadow

STAN GALLOWAY

THE GREAT BELL TOWER OF LAVRA

Nearly as tall as a football field is long
known for not its bell but the sound of its clock

Four stories
    stages of life
    standing one atop another
    on its Dorian
        Ionic
        Corinthian legs
spirited forward from those long-dead Greeks

Stern *baba* watching over all Kyiv
in celebration
    starlight
    tears

Heart stopped just once in 1941
revived to herald borrowed breaths

Body chimes every fifteen minutes
marking the air with
the brevity of time
remaining for repentance

ADELE GARDNER

RISIBILITY

Our Dad is a laugh connoisseur:
Strong guffaws in our clan, de rigueur;
    He'll start a laugh riot
    When it gets too quiet,
Like a cat's inclination to purr.

With our hoots and our screeching long howls
We might be parliamentary owls;
    With our barks, roars, and neighs
    As we cackle away,
We're as wise as the beasts and the fowls!

Giving in to our whinnies and brays,
Shrieking laughs make our ears ring for days.
    With my unicorn-trumpet
    And Dad's rhythmic floor-thump, it
Might be a jazz band he's raised.

Funny papers or morning cartoons,
Four kids whoop in Dad's armchair like loons.
    Puns and punchlines so sly
    And that look in his eye
Stitch us up into helpless cocoons!

There's a wit to this light-hearted man;
His hilarity comes with a plan.
    His joy is contagious:
    A cure for what plagues us,
So let's laugh, and stay young as we can!

Adele Gardner and Delbert R. Gardner

Gold Hill
for Marilyn

Sitting where we joined our lives as one,
I try to get some writing done while you
And Mother, and two of our children,
Go to the "end of land" to visit kin.
The air up there is more rarified, and although
I am no stranger to rarefied air—
Neither are you, my love; together
We've reached the heights full many a time—
I think sometimes of John and Louis,
Who helped me explore the nuances of Hamlet's
Soliloquy at 3:00 a.m. in a coffeehouse—
The figurative interpretation, but now my
Literal lungs insist upon a certain amount
Of literal oxygen with every gulp of air!
A presence walks across my field of view:
Tall, nearly as tall as a man, but four-legged—
A hornless deer—could be a young buck or doe,
Ambling through the backyard in search of food.
It looks at me, decides I'm not a threat,
And hunkers down by the wall in the corner of the yard.
Is there a moral here? If I don't go to the wild,
The wild will come to me!
       Rarefied air, yes—you and I have known
No dearth of that! The time we stood atop Gold Hill
And pledged our love was just the beginning.
The night we drove through Loveland Pass
At 12,000 feet, nervous all the way upon
Precarious winding roads with sheer drops
Of several thousand feet right beside
The two-way road cut through the Rockies—up,
And up and up and up, the evening's drive
Soon turned to agonizing tunnel vision
On that too-narrow road as twilight turned,
Night needing all my courage to focus on
The road that twisted from the mountain's base.
You, dear, looked down in wonder, pointing out
The lights that snaked below us on the hill
From cars and distant houses; said in awe,
"Look how far down it is."

            My hands on the wheel,
Sweating. "Let's not talk about it." But I marveled
At that immensity of space, unbracketed by guardrails,
The paved road raw-cut through the mountainside.
That air, so rarified, required measured breaths—
Good thing. It kept me calm. Thank God it didn't storm!
And yet that air felt just as electrified
As the sharp charge before the lightning comes.

We've weathered many storms. Once, long ago,
Your parents weren't sure I was the man
To match your brilliant life and keep you safe.
They warmed to us with grandchildren and time.
Patience, the key to everything: and your love.
Through layoffs, working many jobs, long hours,
The move down South, and other moves besides,
We always managed to return to Boulder,
To reunite with your family, whom we loved,
And drink again delicious mountain scenes,
Reminding us of your brother's Honeymoon Car,
The red convertible he loaned us for our wedding
At the Little Church in the Pines near his rugged house
Where I stayed before the wedding, and the cabin
Owned by the family of his future bride
Where you stayed with mother, sister, sister-in-law,
Before that joyful day when we embarked
On vows, on life together, and drove to the top
Of Gold Hill farther up the mountainside.

Today, the same as when we stood astride
Gold Hill in awe of rugged peaks of white
And pledged the love that had begun beside
A rounded lake when we danced with delight,
We say, "Some things last; our love will abide."

James L. Garrett

The Guesser

The shorter days had stolen warmth from last month's sun.
Sightseers now spent less time around the aged boardwalk
and spending even less time about his guessing booth.
His summer earnings as with others had taken a fall.
He suddenly experienced a twinge, he guessed,
of doubt about leaving his booth and all the fun.

Too soon the booths would close to tourists and all their fun;
the owners seeking milder climates in the sun.
He had chosen not to return as Dave "the Guesser"
to entertain the passers-by along the walk.
For forty years, Dave had guessed summer to fall
delighting young and old at his aged guessing booth.

Amazed, the many families who visited the booth
would stand in line for Dave to guess their ages for fun.
He was possessed with memory that seemed infallible;
there were no second guesses in Playland sun.
The visiting strollers now came less often to walk
amid the fair-like atmosphere to jazz "the Guesser."

Details were instantly recalled to help him guess
her age as she stood smiling shyly at his booth.
He judged the smoothness of her skin, the way she walked.
Defeat "the Guesser" and win a trinket for your fun:
some colored bands, a shiny bangle for the sun.
But now, the sun was slowly sinking into fall.

The funny man with glasses felt now the touch of fall.
So many years, not often had he missed a guess;
but, when he did, his friendly smile became the sun.
His smile and his garrulity imbued the booth
with gaiety as he made his concession fun.
The guessing man was popular on the boardwalk.

Amusement booths were closing up and down the walk.
The day was slipping past and soon the night would fall.
His time was almost done, and so, with it the fun.
The last of the Mohicans had departed, he guessed,
and now the time had come for Dave to close his booth;
to bid so long this Palace Playland in the sun.

The day had lost the sun as Dave began to walk
away from his aged booth into the days of fall.
He hazarded one last guess: there would be no more fun.

Children of the Sun

From lands across the Atlantic,
from their "home of the sun"
to Savannah shores
the Tosyoha had come.
Descendants of the Lucayans
and known as the Yuchi,
they had lived a millennium
in a coastal area now submerged.
These Children of the Sun.

They founded a town; called it Yuchi;
under protection of the Creeks.
They lived southeast of Columbus
on the banks of the Chattahoochee.
A *Taliwa*, daughter village, was built
away from Yuchi Town
on fertile land beside Uchee Creek—
a new settlement was begun.
These Children of the Sun.

The Children of the Sun
had gray eyes, a light complexion,
and spoke a different language
from other Indian tongues.
The Yuchi hunted the wildlife
that thrived along the creek.
They hunted deer and fox—
better hunters than the Creeks.
These Children of the Sun.

In 1814, at the Battle of Calabee Creek,
Yuchis led by Timpoochee Bernard
turned the tide against the Red Stick Creeks,
saved Gen. Floyd and his Georgia militia.
Now they faced a tougher foe
in the white man's desire for land.
After the Creek and Seminole Wars,
Old Hickory said, "They'll have to go."
These Children of the Sun.

Pres. Jackson gave the direction,
and the government drafted a plan.

The Yuchis, descendants of the Lucayans,
would be forever gone from the land.
These Children of the Sun.

Claudia Gary

Catheter Ablation

Two hours on the table
his body reclines
arranged as a path

      for cautery's snake
      to enter his heart.

Clean current stamps
invisible scars
to settle his pulse.

      No longer two steps
      ahead and one back,

blood coursing forward
oxygen-laden
quickens his brain.

      The serpent withdrawn,
      he gathers his wisdom.

Aunt Rose

Young ladies in their rubber bathing caps
swim measured strokes across the basement pool
of the Barbizon Hotel. Not an ear, not a curl
is visible. Their strong-legged kicks resound

as Aunt Rose shows me geometric wall tiles
and ropes of floaters bobbling between lanes.
We stroll next door where blue-clad Peter Rabbit
looks up at me from glossy-coated paper

pressed, bound, and cut. His mouse friends sort bright beads.
A kitten nearly gets baked in a dumpling.
With this month's new book in a crinkly package,
Aunt Rose takes my small hand and walks me back

to her own lobby shop, joining my mother
amid the shelves of thin-boxed shiny nylons.
The dried-off swimmers march in on high heels,
then out again. How straight their stocking seams!

Rose isn't my real aunt but one whose nephew
died in the Navy during World War II,
leaving a girl who would have been his bride.
The young girl pulled together, studied art,

got a job, went to a dance, and found a husband.
They had two baby girls whose ties to Rose
are echoed splashes, chlorine-rubber air,
mosaic tiles, beige silk, synthetic mesh,

and stubby books whose sweet aroma floats
through and around me as I fan the pages.

Balloon Flowers, Memorial Day
Platycodon grandiflorus

Here is your Sunday water, one day late.
Yesterday's motorcyclists thundered by,
distracting me. An oddly patient state
pervades your purple helmets. Tell me why
bikers stormed town, unfastening its rest
en route to Rolling Thunder, bearing faith
to missing war friends. Isn't life the best
memorial? What's this, their 38th?

Your blossoms, "sentimental blue," begin
as palest pentagonal balloons,
then burst on perforated lines too thin
to recognize as patterns or as wounds.

Opened, you gaze in this or that direction
oblivious to noise and imperfection.

Bill Glose

Things Left Unsaid

What I meant to say this morning
as you divvied pills into a plastic case
with slots for days of the week,

was that sparkles dancing on your cheek—
light refracted from the suncatcher
in the window—reminded me of our trip

to Pennington Gap, that steep drive
up the mountain, nosing through clouds
until we kissed the very blue of heaven.

Those were the days of *Yes*,
when we looked past strangling vines
of kudzu to notice the rock face

of a grandfather speaking from a wall of slate,
his shadowed mouth a cupful of promise.
No wonder we stopped at the glass studio

whose sign advertised "Lessons."
Fearlessly, you plunged your
dye-dipped "gather" into the kiln's

glowing heart, furnace hot enough
to transmute bones to chalk.
When you blew into the spinning rod

and molten glass expanded into
a silver-streaked globe, I could tell
you believed anything was possible.

That is what I meant to say this morning
but didn't, staring instead at your hands
as each pill plunked into its proper bin.

Theories of Flight and Forbearance

In the rumbling gloom of a Starlifter's belly,
paratroopers sit shoulder-to-shoulder
in cupped mesh of bench seats, jostling in sync

with the juddering plane as if their mass
were one breathing body, a desert snake
sidewinding over sand. Parachutes on backs

press them into rucks balanced on laps.
Laden like mules and wedged tight
as an M4's detent pin, bodies interlock

like Spartan hoplites at Thermopylae,
like cavalry at Balaclava, like Pickett's
boys racing toward the low stone wall

on Cemetery Ridge. Arrowing toward
uncertain futures, each jumper ponders
drop zone assembly areas studied from

sand tables, markered on maps whose
contour lines mimic ripples on a pond.
Or else they empty minds like a guru,

aware only of the living moment,
serenity coming like sleep without dreams.
Flecked with sweat, grease-painted faces

are stoic as marble busts of Plato or Socrates.
They, too, know the value of asking why,
but S.O.P. dictates silence. Jingling dog tags

must be taped, as if covering blood type
and religious affiliation might blot out
thoughts of ruin. When side doors open,

cool air tongues the suffocating tube.
Jumpmasters swipe bladed hands across
steel lips then lean into the howl of night,

camouflage fabric snapping in spastic glee,
nap of the Earth scrolling by like images
seen through the slots of a zoetrope.

Sticks rise to their feet and each man
snaps his nylon static line onto the wire cable,
surrendering himself to this machine.

When the door's red light turns green, he will do
what is expected—march forward, pivot,
and leap, prop blast throwing him sideways

before silk rights the world again. So easy
under canopy to consider how little control
he has on anything after that first step—

the ever-upward rush of ground,
the topography of fate, the way everyone
is hurtling toward some form of impact.

Dark Matter

Nights when black swallows the moon,
gulps down crescent-bit remainders
reflecting another continent's sun,

emptiness of space yawns into lungs
like comets cresting event horizons,
streaking tails stretching as they slip

into black holes. Copernicus once spurned
religious doctrine to proclaim Earth
spun round the sun, not the other way around.

Now he ponders whether dark matter exists,
an all-encompassing power
impossible to scoop up and study in a lab.

A kind of faith, the way minds fill in
what eyes can't see or hands grasp.
The heart believing that invisible energy

rules our world, spins its axis,
pushes its orbit round a star
we hope will rise again tomorrow.

June Goodenough

Sacred Ground

A fair summer day it is, a soft, quiet gentle place,
green carpet of grass below and above so blue;
warm enough to wear bare feet and a brimmed hat for shade.
Toes tickled, twined in grass grown long.
Bees and birds speak within the green leaves of every tree;
trading places frequently, but never flying far.

I sit me down beside the path on a sagging, time-worn bench;
The oak wood smooth beneath me holds the heat of day—
my eyes close reluctantly.

My closed eyes leak as I lean back and surrender to another day
when we two brothers had come just here.
The pain of breathing smoke-laden air, the stench of waiting dead;
the nerve-fraying screams ever long, or cut deafeningly short;
the percussion of cannons throwing death down yon green hill;
the fading light in your blue eyes as you died beside this path.

Katherine Gotthardt

Cardinal

Mornings, I want to write deeply,
delve into the beak of the cardinal by my window,
pull his routine song into my poem,
make something more beautiful than myself.

Instead, the day gets swallowed,
sits in a full belly where hours and years swell
into reminders we don't get to do
half of what we want to do,
a quarter of what we need to do,
perhaps none of what we dream to do.

See, I have aspirations,
hopes that hitchhike on wings,
land on high branches,
build nests among spring leaves and breezes,
strain to touch the sky's thin edges—
indeed, I'd be able to fly
whenever mood or need arises.
But mostly, I remain grounded.

So for now I borrow a feather,
dip it in red ink and affirmations,
lower that sharp tip
to a page in a mulberry notebook,
quill my words in cursive:
"Still," it says,
"I live."

Marjorie Gowdy

Minié Ball

Roland rustles through johnny grass in September pasture
downhill from the old battlefield.
He faces a rattled barn full of mildewed hay
under sky which watched boys years ago
rush opposing from weighted heights.

Sun rays cast azure on gold until the drums began
and metal clashed
and the flicker flew, fast, toward the Dunker church
as crimson soaked the ground.
Rabbits ran, and fox, but youngsters strapped on boots and stayed.

It's a funny thing, thinks the old man. *We never talked about the wars.*
Nothing to be gained. But just over the hill here
when I was twelve we rummaged and wrestled,
we watched stock cars screech on clay and drank orangeade
under the walnut tree.

We found minié balls and pocketed them, to show the girls.
It'll kill you, Pop used to say. *A minié ball goes straight*
to the bone. Shatters.
They'll cut your leg off.
If you live.

Roland pushes back a white strip of hair, cleans his glasses.
At ten, our backs bare on dewed evening grass, catching catfish.
At eighteen, the Pacific.
At ninety-eight, this field. Alone.
He rests on the slope as dark sky clambers up a far Allegheny ridge.

He arranges his treasures. The minié ball he gave Helen.
The arrowhead she gave him, lace-wrapped smell of her.
The broken bayonet pulled from a groundhog's hole.
Summer's end, fescue fingers fall over in the heat.
Stalks stand in clay. Red river streams over weary weeds.

Winslow Homer painted war. Imagined hues revealed rusting shades of blood.
My grandson's gone, and with him, our treasures:
the bent silver lure,
the orange bottle caps.
Tulle tinted by supple skin as she turns her head to greet him.

China Alice

Ten miles straight west,
bird flies from this valley to Head of the River Church.
Tucked toward rear headstones, China Alice. Asleep one hundred years.

Plateau-top, creeks run two ways, ribbon road down the mountain.
Dark beauty, that thick black-stump hair, courted by a mischief man.
China Alice keeps a finch in her parlor.

Farm seasons. Plow in March. Sow in May. Harvest in August. Cook.
Bread wafts through a bent kitchen screen.
Pickles. Tomatoes. Pole beans. Butter by Mabel, churned.

A slight figure in gingham, steaming out of the pan-heated tub,
slings back her braids, pulls on slip of skirt,
sneaks out to the shed for a peek.

What does China Alice think of this wanderer four generations down,
late in life come home? The prodigal
feeding wary wrens, seeking quiet now that the flash is gone.

Black-veiled granny sends the bird
back down the rock-strewn cliffside with a message:
Stay.

ORISON

Two scores keening
You now would be sixty
Wise, calm soul, tree-tall and slim
Shyness veiled by a crooked smile.

They called the eve of all hallows
You tried to save the house
Your fingers gripped the red metal tube
You sank helplessly in fumes.

Luminous family brilliance
Chance inheritance of sorrow, too
The night your eyes turned blue
Boy in seizure, frame lifted to the sun.

The portents
That winter, you reported the old man danced on his casket
That summer, our shoulders weighted by ancient quilts
That fall, a few days before, we swore to seek joy.

We carved a pumpkin on the round brick steps
You carried my little son your likeness
I sense your visits on solemn nights the smell of smoke
I wish it had been me.

Lyman Grant

Toward Atonement
   Three images from a novel by Marilynne Robinson

A good first step is to purchase a houseplant,
say, a geranium, and place it on the dusted desk

by the window of your shabby room. Ah,
that afternoon light flat upon the open palm

of its leaves! Tend to it, like a child, lean
close and smell the citrus of its happy innocence.

Next, once you know you will not kill
the bloom, find the tiny book your father gifted

you before you fled, so many pages with folded
corners and question marks. Feel once again

the press of his hand on your knee, the sounding
of his fear for you, sinking, sinking, in his always

forgiving watery eyes. Retrieve that favored
passage and ask those perfect words to haunt you

again, and again. It is you, not he, who dreads
the returning. The shutter, the quaking in your chest,

are aftershocks of a greater distant slippage.
Finally, pick up from the floor the letter, soiled

and stained by its long journey to you. Yes, now.
Now you commit, before the tear and the unfolding.

CLOUDY DAY

It should have been easier
to lift from the chair and walk
the neighborhood today. Stillness
insisted that lives be at ease,
and almost I did not listen.
But once in the street, descending

from the house toward the park,
I felt the flannelled air of gray
sky hug me, enwrap and enrapt
me, steadying something very
wobbly inside. What if I had not
seen my gardening friend Cathy

kneeled in her front lawn kindly
planting bulbs for the coming year,
had not heard the voices of young men
playing basketball rise to enchant
me in their sweetly masculine
exuberance, or couples laughing

on a porch, drinking wine, playing
an old folk tune on their guitars,
the rising minor key chiming
the falling leaves, carnelian,
gamboge, and maroon? How emptied
would I have remained, bereft

of pots of xantic mums alighting
front steps, or jagged-toothed pumpkins
smiling as I sauntered by, giant
maple leaves crusting and crackling
under my feet? Turning the final
corner near home, I find the neighbor's

wild ageratum misting her lawn
in wistful mauve starbursts. And this
was fifteen minutes I could have
lost, negligent, when tender
majesty was so close, and
beauty's comfort offered so free.

David Habib

Milagros

There's no room left on my father's cross.

Let me explain:
they're called *milagros*,

small wishes
pinned to something that means something—
in this case, that shape that one could nail his hands to
(for example)
to summon strength, or to resist some demon's.

We don't know how he came by his miracles
(that's what *milagros* means, miracles)

maybe at some rustic chapel,
itself suitable for framing,
or (more likely)
at a Texan tourist trap

>   [POLONIUS, *aside*]:
>   How did I put it?
>   Tragical-comical-historical-pastoral.

You see he doesn't really know his children,
let alone his relics,
anymore.

>   [POLONIUS]: He remembers less and less.
>   A rain shadow.
>   But he spins bright gold from straw,
>   and he'll offer cake, if there's cake or not.

The cross remains against a wall, a mystery.
And like I said
there's no room left on there

and anyway,
though we searched and searched,
there's no more miracles.

SAQQARA

> "Now Ariel, I am that I am, your late and lonely master,
> Who knows now what magic is: the power to enchant
> That comes from disillusion."
> "The Sea and the Mirror," W. H. Auden

I know now what magic is:

not the capsules in the cabinet,
or the purpose of a mill-pond.
The ruined spine of my Ulysses.

> (everyone
> below these sands
> is lying
>
> names are hammered over names—
> here and there a sacrament.
> a long-forgotten trick of light,
> a striking blue
> in relief)

Here's our power:
when we touch the work
of others,
a wave collapses.
A thousand years, an instant.

> (tell my son, if I am gone)

To see the stars correctly
you have to wait till dark.

I know what magic is:
the latest brief experiment of stones
digging for itself beneath the sand.

Alexandra "Zan" Delaine Hailey

Vincent, out of Doors
Looking at Vincent Van Gogh's "Bedroom at Arles"

Away from Paris, farther south,
the sun beats stronger tangerine
strokes on white lilac—scoring
colours of the prism, veiled

in mist; before western skies
flower red. *I take revenge*
on my bedroom with tilted brushes.
A wicker-backed chair, unsittable

against the closed door embedded
in royal washed plaster, facing
its wooden partner, who sits patiently
beneath an out-bent window,

lit by Number Two Chrome
that brightens a small collection
of polished sketches—bowed copper
wire, dangling silhouettes—above

my periscoped bed frame, where
sleep fractures vibrant oils
on blank canvas. Think, more
Japanese. *A single blade*

of grass; verdant concave, veins
scaffolding a rooted spine. *Simple*
as buttoning your waistcoat.
Rays horizontal blue

brazing cobblestone streets,
where violet figures pattern *a host*
of new subjects—night prowlers—
with indigo strolling shadows.

Words in italics, borrowed from Vincent Van Gogh's letters to his brother
Theo.

Praying Mantis

Ridges ladder a slender
back perpendicularly lined
in burnt orange—he sways,
swinging forearms like a jazz

man on keys before stopping
to stare at a file folder
reflecting his delicate lime-
green structure; sweet sax
radiates through radio

before purifying white walls
with a touch of liveliness
right out of Robinson's back
lily garden: tips dripping

orange neon from golden
nectar breasts. Mantis's serrated
limbs climb to the ceiling
exploring spackled foam-core
that holds fluorescents in place—

the withered gleam, never
as warm as lamp light, works
for now, just as a picture speaks
so many words but never

does the moment justice,
relative to presence. A triangular
face waits patiently for clocks
to strike release—freedom
from stone walls that fracture

each passing day. Ink-crossed
calendar blocks roll, finding
fresh cycles endearing
and repetition swelling. See,

it isn't time that changes
people; people change time.

The Clock Maker

softens sanded faces
smooth for winding hands to glide
cycles—clouds to core,

traces space-time, marked—
circumbing arched-increments'
penumbrous tocks;

falls back resetting
today's path, to linger with
the afternoon sun,

asks what makes bodies
tick in autumn warmth before
stem cells rebuild hearts

stemmed glasses clink across
cherry knots, in crystal rays.

Cathy Hailey

Passage through the Sinks
Great Smoky Mountains National Park

As I watch you prepare to leap
from twenty feet of Smoky Mountain rock,
I understand your hesitation, your search
for courage to force the next step.
The cascading water beckons you,
as it did me a decade prior,
through the cavernous underground passage
it created below the surface in the rock.

Relief comes to me as you step back,
relax your muscles, shaking out your arms,
and Dad takes your hand.
Together you step closer to the edge.

Go alone or don't go, I think, someone will get hurt.
Dad steps back, takes the glasses from your head,
the sandals from your feet, and you approach again,
your toes inching for the edge of golden rock,
thirsty for the chill of the mountain sinkhole.

I feel you take a breath and urge yourself to go,
but you remain, toes clenched, hands fisted, still daunted.
When the others appear behind you
to await their turn, I lose hope and claim relief too soon,
thinking you'll retreat, but instead they spur you on.
Your backstage moments come to an end,
you hold your nose to make your entrance
and jump, propelling yourself into the icy pool,
with little splash and much applause.
The others, older, perhaps wiser, follow suit,
while you climb the colossal cliff to jump again.

A Doll and a Dream

She's a doll in her square-necked dress, high heeled pumps,
bright dark brown eyes, red lipstick smile across her face.
She enters the party New Year's Eve, last day of 1955,
and sees her dream speeding across the foyer to meet her.

It's all documented in eight-millimeter film by cousins
who threw the party, hoping to match up Greek DC gents
with unmarried young ladies in Cedar Grove, New Jersey.
He introduces himself as he takes her hand, leads her away.

Music and dancing rage downstairs in this split-level home,
and that's where they spend the evening dancing to Glenn Miller
and his orchestra—"In the Mood," "Moonlight Serenade,"
"That Old Black Magic"—bewitching each other as they dance.

He leads her across the room, dipping her with a sweet kiss
to celebrate a promising new year, a brighter future—
frequent visits to her Montclair home, Packard drives
to Eagle Rock, dinner dates, carriage rides in Central Park.

Photographs document an engagement party crowded with cousins,
buffet of homemade Greek delicacies, honey-filled desserts, Greek
Orthodox wedding at New York's Holy Trinity Cathedral, reception
with orchestra and opera at the bronze canopied Fifth Avenue Hotel.

Enchantment continues on their honeymoon in subtropical Bermuda,
where they rock the Elbow Beach Hotel, winning a jitterbug contest,
then extending their stay at a New York journalist's guesthouse
where they eat grilled steaks and toast to a future life of happiness.

The doll and the dream fade when they bid farewell to New Jersey,
a more difficult life ahead beginning in a row house in a DC suburb,
where sharing a home with a mother-in-law challenges every day.
Still, I take pleasure in seeing the spark of their magical Jersey start.

WIND AND RIVER

Last night's rain amplified sounds of flowing water
in the early April morning, audibly transforming Rattlesnake Creek,
winding around behind our house, into a rushing river.

Still, the sun made a bold appearance, drying pavement,
rosebush leaves, and tulip petals; warming us as we drank
tea and coffee with whistling finches and a sparrow serenade.

When the wind picked up, rising to a howl, then subsiding,
it sounded like ocean waves crashing on the shore
and we dreamed of squeezing together, nearly touching,

sharing sandwiches and sodas on the beach,
the way we did on family vacations, joining
cousins in Point Pleasant Beach, New Jersey.

Back home, a storm was clearly brewing, but raindrops
only stippled the landscape before the sun beamed bright.
The wind screamed in anger without retreating,

yet I refused to withdraw into the stillness of the house.
I'd rather join forces with wind and river, feel the spiritual
kinship that might restore my faith in future's promise.

Mary Mallek Haines

A Game Board

I.
A father bets heavily on his son,
the mother prone to equal bids.
A thrifty dad, ours shunned money
talk. But how he sang, happy
on whiskey sours:
   I wish I were single,
my pockets would jingle. I wish
I were single again.

II.
In Antonia Fortress Roman soldiers
engraved a game board in stone—
each move a reminder.
They rolled dice
for the Rebel's crimson cloak.

III.
A mother divided herself among
her children, but like an orange
shared, not always equal
the division, not always sweet
an investment. She has yet to retrieve
   her thought, her vision.

IV.
That each of us dies
for love is poetry enough.

V.
The father wagered on the son's fall.
Surely he knew where the mother would
stand, looking up at broken flesh.
   Tears kissed the ground
and the earth shook, before it opened.

Mother stepped out Christmas Eve
wrapped in her beaver coat—
          ungraceful exit:
the living room beribboned in reds,
a gold drift and blur

years cannot focus. Night of *Wigilia,*
opłatek, the holy wafer we broke
          and shared. *Kalendy* half-sung.
Only snow under the pole light,
          its full and certain clarity.

Where did she store the secrets,
where learn to sequester
          life from her progeny?
To sort and fold by color, genre,
degree of delicacy?

Seasons revolved around Mother,
wavering as she did
          that night in Daddy's study.
Snow globe still,
but around her
we, all five, in her orbit swirled,

waiting for a sign,
unable to settle
          the ragged edge of grief:
her mother meeting death that night,
and we not invited.

Without Brakes

Water buffaloes' gray imprint—wading
        into rice fields, an afterthought.
Smoke plumes and the train carves a gentle S

through the hills. A switchback. Washboard
        Arizona road, sienna red.
The joint between old and new, a patchwork

pavement's rhythm. Why hearing? the last sense
        to leave. A train's less-than-perfect
union with the rail resonates, decelerates

                all the way to first heartbreak.
Whistle's moan. Loves spent. Eventually everything

unfettered.   Oh, nights the train coasts
        into depot. Only a crisp attendant
moon. The heart non-stop, never losing

momentum. When I breathe my final, I want it
        to be like yours, like a train slowing
at a new outpost, coasting without brakes.

PHYLLIS HALL HAISLIP

MOM'S POWER

You know the sun will rise.
But in the anxious hours before dawn,
you wonder if darkness will endure
and day can really separate from night.

Multiple births happen every day.
But in the anxious hours
before the arrival
of the eternal miracle,
you wonder if this time
the births will go all right.

One day the womb
is dark and within an hour
two eyes squint at the light,
two others close tight.

Fully formed, tiny, precious,
healthy, hapless new life,
rest now in Mom's loving arms,
she who separated day from night.

First Love

His uncombed, dark hair,
his clenched fists,
his startled, defiant look
won my heart.
I saw beauty
in his blotchy, red face.

A bruise like a smear of lipstick
scarred his forehead.
He thrust out his bottom lip
in an angry cry.
I cradled him in my arms,
soothing him with
tender words and kisses.

His head lolled
against my shoulder
as he settled into my embrace.
Collapsing
like a bean-filled toy,
my newborn son relaxed.

Susan Hankla

I'm not Evelyn
Three excerpts

One Hundred Years of Solitude saves me.
Because of it, I break with my will-o-the-wisp,
and search for brain light, for color, for a place to sit.
Sometimes a rainbow shows at the edges
of mirrors as we raise the hem of the dress
that monarchs land on—this garment my good aunts sew.
In the surrounding fields, I steal cantaloupes and corn,
as place to place, I hurtle,
an endangered village
inside my mouth.

***

If you are missing something, someone, anything,
look at flowers. They are the same as the ones that kings
have seen. Buttercups slick inside the mouths of mastodons in a field.
And peonies, sweet peas & Queen Anne's lace in the silver vase,
in the sick room, by the side of the road my aunt stopped
the car so she could pick handfuls. Orange trumpet flowers, jasmine,
honeysuckle nursing bees. Altar flowers of glads and chrysanthemums.
And magnolia blossoms, waxy on each windowsill for the visitation.
Remember to sign our Guest Book before you leave.

***

Always write w/scented ink in pens that resemble flower stems
with flowers flopping at the ends.
Play with paper dolls called family.
Wear the mountaineer hat with your name
in silver glitter from the State Fair when you write.
Bring home the Angora rabbit and some jelly.

Warren Meredith Harris

Theology at Eighty Miles an Hour
July, 2002

On I-64 between Richmond and Highland Springs,
a woman about thirty with her cigarette glowing in the wind
careered past me on the right in a rust-ruined
Nissan hatchback stuffed with the sum of her things.

The rear windshield disclosed "Jesus on Board."
Why not? He wouldn't need to compete
with boxes, TV, and flapping clothes for a seat
and would blush in a Lexus, this donkey-traveling Lord.

Does he ride with the prudent barricaded in a Volvo
and not with a soul reckless of death and the morrow?

Haiku for the Metrorail

Race past the platform
motionless—to your seatmate:
absolute Einstein.

Dylan's Places
Homage to Dylan Thomas
Wales, February, 2000

Slight, wavy-haired, rude, some said absurd,
you killed many a pint in pubs, and many an hour,
from Swansea to Mumbles to Laugharne, getting bleary and slurred.
I hunted some of these sancta. They were smoky and sour,

with a sport broadcast or incessant music blaring.
Spruced-up Romeos traded alcohol vapor
with smiling women, to the pinball's beeping and glaring.
What had these dens to do with what you put on paper?

I know you had a refuge, sober and green,
where you heard the cascading of a poppy's protoplasm,
the muffled trickle of a subterranean stream,
the rustle of petticoats in a hedgerow, the swineherd's spasm,

the sighs of disappointed lovers, the shrieks of birds,
and the ticking of starworks, in a pure bacchanalia of words.

CLAY HARRISON

PEACE

"Peace is not something you wish for,
it is something you make."
Kayla Mueller: ISIS hostage killed in Syria

Peace is not something you wish for,
it is something you make.
It's a dream you keep on dreaming
even when you're awake.
Peace is the way you treat others
regardless of race.
It's a simple act of kindness,
a smile on your face.

Peace reaches across borders,
welcomes strangers next door.
It gives hope to the homeless
who arrive on our shore.
Peace is the silver lining
behind the darkest cloud.
It's the calm voice of reason
that quiets angry crowds.

Peace is love put into action
when faith leads the way.
It's compassion in its purest form
for those we meet each day.
It's sharing our resources
giving more than we take.
Peace is not something you wish for,
it is something you make.

BOSTON STRONG
Boston Marathon, April 15, 2013

The Ides of March are over,
Easter has come and gone;
and on this lovely April day
we entered the unknown.
Thousands lined the streets of Boston
to watch the marathon,
an American tradition
that continues on and on.

They came from many nations
with dreams all their own,
for in the midst of huddled masses
each runner runs alone.
A sudden blast, a cloud of smoke,
a shriek, a cry, a moan
followed by a second blast
and precious dreams were gone!

Newlyweds each lost a leg;
the winds of war had blown.
An eight year old had lost his life,
his sister's leg was gone.
The unimaginable had happened;
we entered the unknown.
Evil never takes a holiday
but hope lives on.

Wendell Hawken

Within the Confines of this Pasture
How the Universe is Understood

Pitch-black mornings, I leave the lights off so I can see
to find the horse out in his field,
his dark shape darker than the dark.

Rope and halter in my hand, ankle-deep in tall grass dew, I walk
to where he might be at his rock outcrop
or rump up to his poplar.

A last few crickets sound like memory, so faint I pause to listen—
yes, it's not my mind.
And look up there at all those stars.

There are people who can name each Castor Pollux cluster
and take their tiny boats to navigate
vast black holes of thought through clouds

of dust and gases, spinning disks of planets circling a star
to say we come from hydrogen,
helium, exploding stars,

and that new science is not just genius but the luck of being
in the right field at the right time
with a lead shank in one hand

after trudging through the predawn fog to whistle, listen for a sign,
the tear a horse's teeth give grass, shuffled hooves
as he steps out of the dark, at any second now,

the old horse will and drop his nose into my hand
and let himself be found.

Question

When the white bird comes,
when the secret of wheat
uncovers itself and a terrible
beauty takes up with time
to dance past the glass house
damaged by stone, the owl will
fill the bare fields of night
with her question, always

her question. What else can she ask,
can be asked of herself
and of you who hear through
the maze of your ear nestled
flat on the side of your head,
thin as a shit-eater's grin,
the leer of its learning
the secret of wheat, the kernels of truth
from the seeds of her head—
where else are the dead
to be sprouted?

Aubade

Our horses in the gooseneck,
we're in this capsule of a truck cab
headlights probing thick fog, hurtling through time
and space between white and double yellow lines.
Good way to hit a deer, he says. *They move around
this time of morning.*

Bulldozers decorate a field like toys left out all night.
Cows are chocolate drops.
Creeks and ponds rise white with dreams,
warmer than the air. *Should be scent this morning.*
Though we both know there's no for sure with scent
until hounds try.

If I say the green and gold-streaked fields seem
painted with a palate knife, he would say
Looks like half-dried soybeans to me.
We sit quiet as couples at paper placemats
who pass the salt in silence, know to set
the shaker down for luck.

I watch familiar slide by unfamiliar in the fog.
Not as quiet as it looks on a Sunday morning 6:00 AM,
radio praising *Jesus as my savior, you take him too*
hauling horses across the county
to help exercise West Loudoun hounds,
his right hand resting on his right thigh
fingers spread, the way he sits to drive or ride
while I look out for deer.

Neva Herrington

A Family Chair

Sent to me, its inheritor,
the eighteenth-century maple chair
emerges from a five-foot carton
more character than furniture:
the grip of downward-curving arms,
the slightly forward-tilting posture

from metal treads on the back legs,
inclining the chair's occupant
toward family clamor, mine, the day
I asked my father what he lived for,
and as if in the chair he could give
no other answer, he said, "My children."

I once heard in a museum
a Congo people's funeral trumpets,
wooden horns as family icons
to encourage their dead's contented presence.
This chair in its seated silence
makes room for my own to enter.

Namesake

The leaves of the geranium I named
for her are curled up like her hands
the night of her heart attack, a sign,
the nurse said, she was giving up.
But she let death go that time.

So this geranium, four years ago
all leaves when I invoked
her spirit on its behalf, scared
if nothing changed, eternity
might also have its boundaries,

shortly flowered in such abundance
friends noticed. Now these stiffened stems
look past treatment as usual,
at risk to prove her here in a flower,
performing for joy in the world.

Breakdown with Starlings

That winter every afternoon
the starlings came for bread. They ate,
then flew away in one body.

I watched them from a bedroom window
in a small, rented house. That winter
I didn't throw bread to birds.

No cure can be single and sure
as starlings flying. Every day
that winter my yard was light as bread.

JANICE HOFFMAN

ON VIEWING MICHELANGELO'S *PIETA*

His *Madonna and Child*
makes us smile, remember
birth and innocence,
the joy of children,
but this statue evokes tears.

She sits there, son in lap,
Mater Dolorosa,
Mother of Sorrows,
and those of us who also
have lost sons relate.

As she does, we remember
our toddling child,
our young teen,
our grown man. We walk
our own *Via Dolorosa.*

For 500 years, this famous
artwork honors our grief
as the sculptor's mallet
and chisel have carved
through marble and

released a mother
contemplating her dead son,
the way I did when I last
saw you and I kissed your
stone cold forehead.

Stones

England, Scotland, Ireland, Wales—
all connected with swirling stones.

In bluestones of Stonehenge
and rock circles of Orkney,
Neolithic magic rings out,
predates pyramids of boulders.

Newgrange graves, Maeshowe's
chambers, and primeval passages
of Great Britain and Ireland's
triple spirals reflect infinity, eternity.

Sun-illuminated dark passages
astronomically aligned assured
longing for and promise of Helper
to hunters and then to farmers.

Ashes and smoke blew
from stone monuments to the heavens
beyond our place in Earth
and into the cosmos.

Who knew that, when my preschool
daughter tossed gravel on the road
and my toddler son scooped pebbles
from the ground, they were

merging with ancient ancestors
beyond time and distance,
wind and air, embracing stones?
Who today understands?

Yesterday, today, tomorrow—
Stone circles matter.

RUTH HOLZER

A WEDDING IN FAR HILLS

We have added our
redundant gift to the heap.

Now my seed-pearl purse lies in the grass.
My new high heels are smeared with mud.

The rented string quartet releases
an adagio to the autumn breeze

and the guests swivel around
in murmurous anticipation

as the groom treads the silken path
to the bower of roses and awaits

the arrival of his bride, conveyed
by her widowed mother, who is

sniffling over the departure
of her only child. The veil is lifted,

the rings slipped onto tremulous fingers,
the kiss prolonged to hearty applause,

and under the heel of the husband
an unmatched glass is crushed.

THE OPEN ROAD

Choking hot on the day-long drive,
but at least I didn't get killed or maimed
on the Beltway or the Interstate
or the Turnpike or the Parkway.

I only bumped somebody's bumper
ever so gently, in a rest stop parking lot,
and no one was in the other car.
Caught a break. On the radio,

New York was beating Detroit
to clinch the Division title,
the star closer splintering bats to glory.

I handed over
the last of my greasy singles
and bolted from the final tollbooth.

MONIQUE

Monique, Monique,
the finished product
of fruitful generations:
almond-eyed, honey-skinned,
a skim of caramel and cream.

You blend the best of everyone:
Mohican, Black and Mexican,
Creole, Irish, Japanese—
an ineluctable allure.

Like your mother
before you, who ran off
with your father, like
your bold grandmother
who eloped with her lover—

ah, Monique, Monique,
suave seventeen,
delicious daughter, you
long drink of water,
you're pregnant too.

BETH SIMPSON HUDDLESTON

RUN, MEADOW, RUN

In the early hours
of dawn, I awaken
to the gurgling rhythm
that draws us back
to a mother's womb.

I listen—
trying to make sense
of your sound combinations;
odd to find message
in something so established.

How immense
to know existence rests
in a myriad of droplets
from the azure-blue hills—
astonishing droplets that carry
with them pieces
of a cataclysmic spirit.

You move swiftly through
our lives, on to others.
Pity that we must absorb
greedily what we
can, while you are here.

Still, your rhythmic
waters are ever-changing,
bring the spirit
of the new,
and carry
away the pain
that to another will be a new,
welcomed experience.

Run, Meadow Run!
Through our souls
as well as our land.

Swell with the floods,
dwindle with the droughts—
always bringing
newness of life,
the soothing
of failure and grief.

Your life and sounds,
the renewal
of our mountain souls.

MARK HUDSON

THOREAU'S FIRE

Henry David Thoreau wrote *Walden*,
a memoir of nature meant to inspire.
Years before he had ended up scalding
the forest, while trying to make a smaller fire.

In Thoreau's home in Concord,
he went fishing with a friend, Ed Hoar.
They had some fish they wanted to cook,
so they set a fire on the forest floor.

They lit the fire over a tree stump,
and watched all the flames tear asunder.
The fire spread fast; they began to run,
to tell the neighbors of this dreadful wonder.

The crackling fire burned all the pine trees,
clouds of smoke rose from the pyre.
They told their tale, between alerts and pleas,
until the neighbors put out the fire.

Thoreau was gossiped about in town,
rumored to be a woods-burning man.
He'd almost burnt the forest down,
while writing *Walden*—his initial plan.

Yes, *Walden* was the book he wrote,
detailing his life in the great outdoors.
The fire he'd created and the damage it smote
are rarely remembered by most, of course.

Luisa A. Igloria

Cargoes

In late afternoon sun, toddlers tilt
forward and back on yard swings
at the halfway home. The high

school girl who volunteers there
wants to know what mother,
what father would throw

a daughter out into the streets, say
Don't come back or *You are as good
as dead to me;* and the middle-aged

woman washing up at the sink looks
through the window at the vanishing light,
startling at the sudden film on her cheeks.

What sifts through the packed soil
as years rush by? Swift as birds in the corn,
long green tassels in the summer evening;

lifted by wind, bearing redolence
of cow manure and honeysuckle.
Along the southbound road,

where the dip rises toward the knoll,
locals tell of a girl who rode behind
her brother on a motorcycle. Who

could have foreseen the truck in the other lane,
its side-view mirror glancing like a blade
along her jaw? The sky's inverted basin

flooding her eyes with the surprise of indigo,
before the head's brittle husk snapped back
and arms and fingers tightened in rigor

around the living body. That's how we press
forward into deepening twilight, carry the shape
of our eternal cargo: the voice that breathes

in our ear saying *love* or *goodbye*—as we
crest the hill and gun to a stop, waiting for the lights
to flash and change from yellow to red to green.

Custody

Chopping cilantro and flat leaf parsley
on a bamboo board at the sink, mincing

garlic and onions. Late mellowing light,
the air bordering on cool but tinged

bitter-green with the smell of growing
amargoso in the yard. I can keep

the kitchen door open because the side gate
is locked, and the weeklong siege at the street

corner is over. We did not know the man
they say trespassed, early Monday morning,

into someone's yard with a firearm;
did not know what altercation if any

led to someone calling the police. So he ran
and barricaded himself in his own house.

They came in force, then; rifles drawn,
sealed off one end of the block. Those of us

who could still come and go out the other end
brought back reports every day, over four

days: how many squad cars, where the waiting
ambulance was parked, the bomb unit; who saw

the robot deployed with a phone, the negotiators,
the TV crew. We did not witness how, before dawn

on the fourth day, finally they took him *into custody*—
from the Latin *custodia* meaning *guardianship*,

keeping care. Now this man who neighbors say
used to pelt their doors with donuts, or attach

stuffed animals on leashes for walks,
is in a hospital or facility. Is it wrong

to wonder if it lasted as long as it did
instead of arriving at swifter resolution—

doors broken in; tasers, clubs; bullets sprayed
into his body—because of the color of his skin?

Or is it possible to believe that finally
something of change might be moving slowly

through the dismal atmosphere, tempering
and holding in check, allowing the thought

to stay the trigger, the heart to register
its trembling before letting the weapon fly?

In summer, because dark descends more slowly,
it's hard to scan the sky for the hunter

and his belt studded with the three telltale
bright stars; harder to remember how

once, he boasted he would hunt down and kill
all of earth's wild animals, to make it safe.

But there he is, adrift in the inky darkness,
club and shield eternally raised, his own K-9 units

at his heels; and here we are, still trying to sort
villain from victim, wound from welcome opening.

Bioluminescence

Article headings flash
on the computer screen. This one
is seasonal: *10 Easy Flowering
Herbs and Vegetables for your Garden.*
I want to plant something windblown
and laden with the smell of yearning,

something that emerges shyly
when the sun goes down.
I live in a house of sheets:
underwear tumbling in the dryer,
blouses of cold water, hand wash
only crepe. The word voile

floats to the surface, voluptuous
and glimpsed only rarely,
swanlike as the neck of the night-
blooming cereus. Studying the shower
curtain and its hems of mold,
little pores on bathroom tile:

I think of green tea sponge cake,
perishable melt of lady fingers;
where to lay out bee balm,
geranium, verbena so as to repel
mosquitoes. The ivy and the fern
want to take over, just like

history. Should I go away
for a few weeks, they'll creep
over everything else. I'd rather
lift the edges to find not sadness
or mist but a velvety limousine; and all
these tiny, winged lights, winking.

Donna Isaac

After Bedtime

A plastic bag held a scuffed and dirty wallet, your gold wedding
band. The police handed these to Mama. The brown wallet, the one
you'd stuff in your back pocket from which you'd hand out dollar
bills, the one that held Mamaw's funeral card etched with an angel
and a stanza of "Thanatopsis," the one your wife gingerly removed,
showing us our school photos inside plastic sleeves, a Moose card,
a Sears credit card, your driver's license, one empty sleeve perhaps
for your unborn son. His name will be Steve after your brother.
Jaws of life cut and peeled the car like a sardine can, the kind you
liked on crackers with hot sauce. In the night, the pop of gravel
rattled our brains, the doorbell, the red rotating light, my mother in
curlers. We moved like robots those days, the summer shrieking hot.

Mississippi Night

A riverboat chuffs and glides,
white lightbulbs strung and lit.

Holiday songs float on air,
cups of kindness raised.

Muck and slush churn through the wheel
like so many viral droplets strung.

Revelers want a safe landing,
an easy passage there.

Will smiling faces candleshine
unmasked and unafraid?

Will dulcet voices sing unbound
the carols of green days?

Laughter peals around the bend,
the hum of engine fades.

Fog enshrouds the weeping trees. The
boat is gone, the river flows hot.

Edison Jennings

Spontaneous Combustion
The Meadows Farm, Abingdon, Virginia

Later, you insisted on calling it a bush, but it was more like a stump,
though sure enough burning where it had gone punky in the middle,
and when you came upon it, you knelt and asked its name,

then took a pull on the flask that maketh glad the heart of man.
The liquor hit and you hollered: "You am? You am what?"
It was mid-May, lambs and ewes in one field, heavy with wool and milk,

rams sequestered in another, butting curled horns, the two of us,
working the meadows, drinking whiskey, mending fence,
sipping fire that maketh glad the heart of man.

Directions to a Ruin

Follow Spoon Gap Road past the Free Will Church
and find a wide-hipped chimney stub
girdled with a snarl of berries, dark and sweet
this time of year, rooted in the fireplace,
blacksmithed pot-hook curled like a come-here finger,
but the house is gone. Lightning burned it down,
the crooked stroke still scarred across the hearth.
In easy view from where a doorway
might have been, several generations lie
beneath a hill toothed with snaggled headstones
tilted by a hundred years of freeze and thaw
where love's observance long ago succumbed
to underbrush and new-growth oak and grief's
alphabet weathered to a palimpsest
on lichen freckled slates. You might rest there,
stretch out in the chimney shade and taste
the wild blackberries, slightly tart with ash.

Cold Spring Morning and the Grade School

Cold spring morning and the grade school
kitchen ladies pack quick-fix meals for poor kids
because the Covid's on a killing spree while they bitch
about the parents because most are probably tweekers,
dopers, drunks, or immigrants ripping off America,
because we give too much away, while a holy DJ shills
Jesus' love for dollars, hawking heaven for donations
so Christ the Risen Lord can feed the poor and hungry,
because their pay is lousy and arthritis spikes
their bones and the grandkids' dad's not married
to the grandkids' mom, so they sneak out quick-fix meals
and no one says a thing because that would be so wrong,
because they have to feed the kids now that daddy's gone to jail
and who knows where the mom is? Maybe she's detoxing,
but the Jesus-shilling DJ is off the air at last,
thank God, and Dolly's singing "Coat of Many Colors,"
and now Aretha raises rafters with "You'll Never Walk Alone,"
and someone mutters amen and another sing it sister and then
as if on cue someone drops a stack of trays and someone
laughs and then a couple more because the righteous racket
is bouncing off the floor, clattering like cymbals,
setting the kitchen ringing, and making joyful noise.

Richard Johnson

Cartagena Excursion

spider webbing
electric live
down across
wide boulevards

wrapping air
wires strung
narrow streets
crumbling façades

tourists photograph
culture fashion
shops set in rows
dealers deal

browse buy
silver gold
seeming safe
hookers hook

hot humid
casts no shadows
flood purgatory
night promise one

midday sun
praying rain
labyrinths moonlit
more *déja vu*

Church in a Meadow

bricks and stones
stained glass shards

fade in ivy
crumble in wccds

gone doors
share a façade

empty windows
frame blue sky

children
share green hills

kites
whisper in wind

Derek Kannemeyer

In Memoriam Richard Fariña
3/8/1937 - 4/30/1966; 3/8/2020, for Jeff Hewitt

I fell hard for him when he was two years dead.
It was 1968. I was 19.
I'd plucked his and Mimi's second album from a discount bin,
then just had to have their first one, and then his novel,
Been Down So Long It Looks Like Up To Me,
the cult classic that kind of killed him.
He died riding the high of a book signing; it had been out two days.
And it was Mimi's 21st birthday, and the perfumes of the spring
were green and wild and hollering, so hey, why not jump
on the back of this guy he barely knew's Harley
and roar about the Carmel hills
about as hard and as loud as that beast could be lashed to go?
Until the death he'd predicted for his pal Bob Dylan
jumped up out of a curve and cold-cocked him.
Great squandered what-might-have-beens, that's his wiki now.
The dude was Dylan's buddy, did you know that? And his bride
was Joan Baez's sister, and Pynchon was their best man.
What-might-have's, and the pan-flash of association.

But I remember a night I couldn't sleep.
It was the end of the 1960s.
I had turned on my bedside wireless and tuned it to pirate radio.
Now *there's* some playback from way back—pirate radio!
It was broadcast from ships offshore, illegal
(the whisper went) even to listen to,
and the signal drifted in and out, which got ghostly, but was very hip.
And at 3 a.m. a song came on I'd never heard—yet it was Richard!
Like a roar from the grave it came: spine-tingling.

I spent decades hunting for that song.
Oh, I found a cover version, and Mimi recorded it solo,
but with Richard singing? That track does not exist. Last week,
when Jeff flew over his handlebars, and all the poems in him
sang scattershot to the ghost winds of the multiverse,
what I heard, for a moment, was the keening
of Richard Fariña's voice out of the ether—
from another plane somewhere—where the impossible glories
of every death too soon
are scooped up and stored on magnetic tape and acetate,
to breathe, if only once, their illicit sweetness, from some vast sea
chest of them, into the far shore seashell of our ear.

Jump Rope Song

Sunrise, sunset, fire on the lake—
my mama wants it, my mama take.
Sundown, sunup, get it while it's there—
my mama one up, yours nowhere.

Where you plan to be when the power grids fail?
Down in the alley, chasing tail?
Crawling round the beltway, snorting gas?
Uptown, downtown, smashing glass!

Jump rope, jump rope, get it while you can,
I'll be your woman if you'll be a man—
high step, low step, stutter step, pass,
how you aim to keep up if you can't smash glass?

Sunrise, sunset, fire on the lake—
my daddy wants it, my daddy take.
Sundown, sunup, get it while it's there—
my daddy one up, yours nowhere.

ROBERT LESTER KELLY

DO YOU REMEMBER?

Do you remember the Senator,
Representative, Mayor, Rector,
droning on under the hot July sun
that drenched us in perspiration
as we stood on the launching stand?

Do you remember Ethel Kennedy
holding the Champagne bottle,
feet apart, Mickey Mantle stance,
smashing it to smithereens,
on the submarine's bow proclaiming:
"I christen thee USS John Marshall?"

Do you remember the Champagne's
heady bouquet filling the air, the
Navy band striking up "Anchors Aweigh"
as Marshall began to move gaining
speed going faster and faster?
7,900 tons of steel sliding down the
shipway, wildly accelerating; its deck
filled with crew in summer whites,
officers in dress whites standing on
the diving planes hanging on for dear life,
finally waves flying high as Marshall
splashes and floats into her salt water home.

Do you remember the reception,
the coolness of the club?
Talking with Ethel and Bobby
just our age, comparing notes
on raising children,
teething troubles?

I remember, Peggy, how beautiful you were,
engaging all with your smile and chatter
while planning dinner for the four boys—
and I, hoping the baby sitter wouldn't be
cross over our boys' exuberance.

Yes, I remember, Peggy,
you, moving like a star
among officers and friends,
enjoying them, beguiling them.

Yes, I remember you, my beautiful,
wonderful, wife, my love.
Yes, I remember.

Michael Jon Khandelwal

Emigrant

She hangs their wash on a bolt
below the passengers who can reckon the horizon,
know how the water bucks this boat against harsh waves.

Steam pushes the hull through an ocean of lost fish;
weeks blur in fog, but she smiles
at the hordes in steerage—the only language they share.

For days now, she's stared at the platform that hangs
above her, dreams to walk the decks of this iron ark,
catch that first glimpse of new land as it looms.

But she knows she must stay with her children, her husband;
everything they own is crowded into brown cases,
and she must carry her memories onto the docks:

the lush warmth of the summer hillside, the night
she wed, surrounded by a village of candlelight,
walks with her mother through fields of fresh barley

when she learned the truth about men. Washing
her husband's face of dried blood. The early morning
when she birthed her first daughter, the pain

of moving life into the world. The scent of paprika
melting in a copper pot, the longing. How she became
her own heat, smoke moving across the hills, across the sea—

Hay Elote

Hay elote, he shouts
outside my window; I have wondered for years
what message he was bringing. Today,
I learned: *there is corn.*
I remember growing
up, seeing rows of cornstalks,
sampling the first of the harvest,
smothered in butter and salt.
Hay elote, the man sings out;
corn, it seems, exists here, too. Perhaps
I am not far from the eastern sunrise,
not far from corn,
feeding us all, in the communion
of hunger for food. The sun is huge
over a field; stalks bristle
in the wind. This man knows,
brings corn to my house, offers
me my mother's hands
in a crowded street.

Grandfather
for Barbara Taylor

Our first meeting, I imagined:
he would see me and then see
himself, and perhaps we would talk
of first love, his second love, a passion
that caused him to leave; my family
never missed him; poetry
is truth and I should not lie: I
had plans to visit him
for five years and did
not; had plans to visit him
later, as he lay dying; I wanted
to see this missing half; I am
too late like I often am and now
there is no history; I will not know
why he left my mother's mother;
I will never hear how
his mother, a Wyandotte Indian,
rode bareback in the early spring;
how the bombs exploded in trenches
as he lay under a German sky;
how he spread his blood to the bodies
of children whose pictures steal my memory.

JoAnn Lord Koff

Illuminations on Ocracoke Ferry

    You are the lone minstrel to my feelings
As I star-wish under you, mysterious moon.
An old, pasty gray face etched in white,
Saying, "Oh!" to whatever I ask of you,
Only crystal clarity, for you cast no shadow.
    So unlike the sun, who warms everything.

    At night, you act like my celestial buoy,
Upon the ocean's jet blackness,
Illuminating the ferry's route across the channel.
Lurking in the deep is Blackbeard's ghost;
Salty sea breezes grab sensibilities.
    So unlike the sun, who warms everything.

    Like a tempest, you dance upon waves
Causing tides to surge in laughter.
Like a silver medallion you outshine,
Disguising all defining shape.
Sprinkling alluring tea lights upon rough surf.
    So unlike the sun, who warms everything.

    Waxing full, I perceive your brilliance,
Under the night sky, I reflect like you.
As you change lunar phases,
You transform the minute to eternal.
Magically giving transparency to thought.
    So unlike the sun, who warms everything.

So

I feel so
obliquely alive;
like a raspberry
pink-poppy
marshmallow,
on a plate
of dried hibiscus.

Sarah E. N. Kohrs

Like Lichen Lingering

Lichen mummifies a silvery tree limb sheening
with drizzled rain, whose murmur mimics
shuffling feet, chained. It isn't the ghast

visage of my son—a visceral cord twining
his neck leeched of ruddy hue, so that perhaps
a moment more, he may never have known a breath—but

the orange jumpsuit of a woman, nameless to me,
who entered the door next door, that haunts
my memory of a birthday. An officer bent to remove

the cuffs on her swollen ankles, then slipped the key
into a starched pocket, waiting and waiting like a gargoyle
placed outside the room. Who held her hand

during contractions or slipped ice chips into her mouth
or simply looked into her eyes as one human to another?
During a birthing day when lime green leaves unfurl

even the breeze seems to sigh. But in such confinement,
alone, a woman becomes the mother society ignores
like lichen lingering on tree limbs sheened with rain.

Into the Depths

I can still remember the day
It's like a stone that skips across the
Pressed into grooves,
of brokenness pull up into
I never wanted to know.

I broke.
pond perfectly.
those moments
a molded form
To know

how the newly rung bell, Liberty,
bound, then, to echoed silence
fluid as aurora that arcs across
(with a different kind of kindling),
even copper alloyed with less.

cracks—
forever. Flame,
the night sky
entrances
With less

clarity, I envision a trail of
sharks twisting into spirals
boarded with black ivory,
stashed in 3-tiered bunks
More left Africa than arrived;

great white
behind bulwarks
clipped & collared,
without straw.
than arrived,

which implies a choice—a choice
by a triangular trade, with faces
meaning. Peer polity interaction
on playgrounds, where bullies
Survival of the fittest, you say?

stolen
maculating mindful
that percolates
abound.
You say,

while flies wield their wings
belched from their pupal shrouds.
wind as it passes overhead in that
Does it resemble the womb's
Or the sound of black holes

about our heads—
What whispers
flickering flame?
solemn rhythm?
colliding? Colliding

into brokenness naïve to joy
a child's laughter from the uni-
I can still remember the day
It's like a stone that skips across the
A smooth stone that sank

as if it never knew
versal peekaboo.
I broke.
pond perfectly.
into the depths.

Red Flecks on a Veneer of Black

Sitting in traffic: slowly moving,
brake lights run rampant. Individ-
contracting [separate] yet mindful
Moving independently, but cogni-
the need to brake. Red lights

the cars'
ually, we're
of one another.
zant of
smolder—

ignite a silent angst. From high
a shimmering molten river: in-
We move like lava in a line—even
light, when the red seems cooled,
by black basalt. At night, when the

above,   we're
flamed // afire.
in the day-
veneered
cars begin

to separate from their pooled den-
appears that bits of flame flicker
expanding just as tea leaves do
angled netting and roving from
They're airlicks made by a slither-

sity, it
up and off,
escaping tri-
the epicenter.
ing snake

or a great, gleaming beast arising
dreams. A beast that doesn't do any-
actifies a gut-deep fear in the mind.
we attribute with something we
and don't want to try to under-

from a child's
thing really, but
A fear
don't know
stand.

We're always searching for the
in the darkness. Our eyes strain
the ethereal in reality: like dis-
of only 8 blood types—a plasma
twines nationalities and should

light
to glimpse
cerning one
that inter-
slow our fear.

Carol Parris Krauss

Pickett's Tomb
Hollywood Cemetery
Richmond, Virginia

Dogwoods stood sentry under the Union blue sky.
Leaned over the carriage paths, war widows
prostrate in mourning. Lace petticoats.

General George Pickett's tombstone stood at the end
of a lane on the cemetery's edge. Circular, solitary.
The clatter of cars crossing Robert E. Lee Bridge

and James River rushes and ramblings,
the only accolades accompanying Pickett in death.
Dirges more palatable than the drops of liquor

that had slowly killed him. Steady sips of pity. Shame.

CAROLYN KREITER-FORONDA

TINNITUS

The ringing like a claw starts,
        a sequestered racket
                that hisses in sleep

and hums in a spring-fed swamp,
        spatterdock's *clair de lune* hearts
                bobbing like vessels.

Easing my kayak beyond the stream's
        fringe, I paddle through
                the after-hush of dusk.

Feverish, the stars. The moon coy
        above a quilt of clouds,
                the wetlands in an uproar—

owls, raccoons, minks sounding
        an alarm as jarring as a howl
                in the hoarse throat

of night. The feathery dark swells
        to a crescendo, a choir
                of spring peepers

in search of mates. Lowering
        my head, I count the times
                their vocal sacs fill

and empty, these cross-bearers
        olive-green, tan and gray,
                colors I see every time

my ear whistles. The din—
        the maddening noise—calms
                among the scent

of half-opened cow lilies,
        seductive in these elusive
                headwaters.

O canopy of bald cypress,
        sycamore, sweetgum,
                dance for me

until my hearing heals
        in the defining hour,
                windless, serene.

Today I Raise The Blinds

on October's gold and red tumblers,
      a balmy breeze clothing
            the brambles, spiders

upside down weaving azure light.
      I open the blinds to see
           the little things:

sun's long legs interlaced
      with soothing birdsong,
           a woodland path

adorned with willowy filaments,
      tidal water moving in
           and out like a tango.

What would I do if this house
      were windowless?
           What would I do

without flame-soaked branches
      of oaks waving
           as wind quickens?

All that color covers the cove,
      a melody of scarlet
           and amber whispering

like a serenade of wind chimes.
      What would I do without
           web-strands guiding

me to the creek, luring me
      to bathe in ripples among
           tumbling leaves?

The first time I saw this piece
      of land, bordered by an inlet,
           I heard the stir and hum

of waves giving praise for small
      creeks hidden from a city's
           thrum and rustle.

Today I raise the blinds and give praise
      for the fluttering *coos*
           of mourning doves

sunbathing far from a nation's wails
      and cries, far from the darkness
           of a disheveled world.

Monarch Survival

Where are the monarch butterflies—
nature's pollinators that once graced
the countryside, their plunge over two

decades sharp enough to threaten
the food supply? What caused this
rapid decline? I search a woodland path,

once laden with zinnias, sunflowers,
and milkweed, the scent of toxic
weed killers permeating the air.

Last year my husband and I raised
and released over two hundred monarchs,
their wings deep orange, black-veined,

the edges bordered with a décor
of white dots. A blessing to watch
them flit among oak branches, dancing

the energetic, wing-lifting jive.
What happened to this rhythmic thrall?
Today across the creek, the blare

of trees pound the earth, resound
as builders strip the land bare to construct
palatial homes, the native milkweed,

the monarch habitat gone. Stand up
for pollinator survival. Stand up.
The butterflies have the right to survive.

Robert J. Krieger

Crossroads at Culpeper

I really tried to wrestle the winter
out of two thousand and fourteen
"submit to this New Year,
and stop being so mean"
my note was of the night
scribbled to my parents, saying,
"the Lone Star is in sight"
grabbing all of my gear,
I opened the door to the dark,
slipping up icy steps,
time to embark!
I dove into the distance,
having faith in Fauquier,
a voyage of insistence,
it was a maddening fifty miles,
as I noticed, "negative nine degrees Fahrenheit"
a temperature of trials,
I called it off at Culpeper,
when someone said to me,
"practice your patience,
approach it with honesty"
I headed home,
but it's not a false start
if you believed in the action
with all of your heart

Joanna Lee

Local Theology
"…and grasps at the hem of heaven." JW

These days heaven, regardless of what the weather report says,
tends to look like the closing credits from an old war movie.

One of those epic panoramics in technicolor, sky-blue-pinks and crimson
yellows—heaven being

always closest to within reach at daybreak—a defiance
to the night's casualties. Coming over the bridge,

you can almost feel the cotton-candy touch of it,
though somewhere along the bank, a dog was shot and killed here

a few dark hours ago. The man who lives with his cat
under the overpass hard by the ramp, having seen so many cold dawns,

could tell you how the new apartments going up
were, not years ago, fields where you'd startle rabbits

with your headlights in the rising sun. Now
workers in neon vests and hard boots knead

weariness into wet cement, showing up every morning
with hands in their pockets. They break the skyline

like a battle… but also the wind. In the relative silence, offer
him a candy bar or better a cigarette

& he'll shake his head between coughs,
like to say all the grasping in the world

ain't gonna bring you
to pinch truth between your fingers

like it was a live thing.

Northside, Richmond

Fat moon slings its shine low, washing the ball courts in Battery Park
a dull aluminum. From where the road transects
the playground, the huge old oak they cut

yawns to the left, its roots leaving deep scars in the clay
like the edge of some wormhole to the underworld.
Like maybe you could disappear there.

Maybe, if you left the road and stepped into the shadow beyond
the yellow caution tape, you could lose
yourself. Maybe,

if you let yourself shed enough of the city,
her catcalls & gunshots & sirens,
her past   & past   & past,

if you left her conflict buried in the cold earth
with the sounds of the corner liquor store
and the squeal of tires into the night,

if you ran your palms
over the rough withered body
of fallen trunk and knew

if dead trees know shame,

you could find yourself again.

Would you come back to her?

Small Mercies

Three blocks from the medical school,
there's a bar with the best cocktail in town.
Your eyes dropped
in your glass,
you paint me autopsies
of infants, politics
of tissue recovery while
I watch the bartender—
short, dark-haired—cut
apart the plastic from a six-pack,
believing, maybe, in its choking
hold on unlucky marine life.
We were all born underwater,
and things *do* get lost in the low light.
Looking out away from the hospital,
at the manicured turf patio, it's hard
to believe anatomists still haunt these grounds.
Poor, apparently, is the new postbellum. Sweeping
the sweat back from his bangs,
he slides us both another. I can't
taste the brand of the bourbon, but,
savoring the char of the rosemary's
smoke, we all three know
it's been one helluva century.

Later, leaving you by your car
in the parking lot-turned burial ground-
turned parking lot again, what I'll remember

is the pretty, marbled veins of the bar top,

is how he cut apart each goddamn ring
with a white-handled knife,

is the evening CSX rumbling overhead,
hard by the overpass, coal
unslowed in darkness, salt-rimmed.

Rebecca K. Leet

Rumination at River's Edge

There's merriment here
where the Potomac's green-brown water

tickles the shore.
Ripples bump and push each other

like a throng of marathon runners
jostling for position at the start of a race.

I wonder about the molecules, each of whose destiny
was to be a dot of a drop in this water—

then to reassemble one day as rain kissing a tulip,
snow falling on the eyelash of a child,

or one in a plump cloud—luxuriously white—
drifting, drifting, drifting aloft.

What of the molecules
whose destiny was to be me?

How will they reassemble
when *I* am no longer *me*?

Will they gather to grace the world
 as a weeping willow, do their duty

as a lowly worm, return to this river
as a great blue heron or a droplet

tickling the shore?

Ebb Tide

As embers of my coal
turn ash,
the final faint draws near,
lay me
where the ocean meets the sand.

Let salt be
my final kiss, the roil of waves
my requiem.
And when the last flicker of rose
turns gray,
feed me to the fish.

Edward W. Lull

Where Giants Walked
Reminiscences while walking on
Duke of Gloucester Street in Colonial Williamsburg

A stroll on this historic street provokes
an awesome sense that here they met and talked.
The sunlight filters through majestic oaks
as reverently I walk where giants walked.
We call them patriots of times long gone;
Virginians all, they shared a common dream.
Their forebears set a standard whereupon
the sons made freedom their enduring theme.

The Capital from sixteen ninety nine,
for eighty years through peace and joy and fear;
this city—Williamsburg—remained a shrine
of liberty, evolving year by year.
As foreign rule increasingly inflamed
the spark of revolutionary thought,
Virginia's leaders forcefully proclaimed
that they would not be bullied nor be bought.

When Jefferson and Henry, Mason, Bland,
and Washington; the Randolphs and the Lees;
and Harrison and Braxton were on hand,
the City hosted greatness: freedom's keys.
Resounding oratory filled the air,
the Capitol, intense with fervent sound.
Debate resumed at Raleigh's Tavern where
the seeds of freedom fell on fertile ground.

The risks were high, but passion for their goal
defeated fear that lesser men sustained.
They formed a Union with both heart and soul,
a gallant victory that brave men gained.
This sojourn down colonial promenade
recalls for me how these men earned renown:
commitment to their cause and faith in God,
where giants walked—in Williamsburg—their town.

C ALLED TO S ERVE

It wasn't called a war, but he was called to serve.
Just months ago they swayed to big band sounds
and promised to share their lives;
but now she saw him off—a soldier far too soon.

He loved her, and he loved the land;
he'd serve his time, then back to Georgia's soil.
He knew that General Doug would keep his word:
win the war and send the boys back home.

To infantry he went—a grunt—as he was called.
His training—very brief—a ship then took him west.
Korea's ice and snow were half a world away
from Georgia's warming sun.

Realities of war were closing on him fast;
his peaceful world would change this bitter day.
His company called to spearhead an attack,
the sickness in his gut confirmed his fear.

Are those we face just farmers much like me,
called to fight for reasons we don't know?
Should I take lives because I'm told I must;
Can I expect God's mercy if I kill?

His squad on point, they squirmed
through bloody snow—he hardly felt the cold.
Grenades and mortars boomed ahead,
while bullets zinged off rocks and icy banks.

Across a ridge he came face-to-face
with a young Asian man in drab gray uniform,
lying on his side, eyes wide in lifeless stare,
gaping hole in his forehead.

Startled and sickened by the sudden encounter
he arose from a pool of his own vomit.
At that vulnerable instant he felt the searing pain;
his thigh was hit with force that threw him down.

He did his best to slow the oozing blood.
MEDIC! MEDIC! He knew he needed help;
the others on the ground were still and cold;
the battle had moved on; he felt alone.

He called again, but felt his voice grow weak;
perhaps some rest would help restore his sapping strength.
His pain had eased, the snow a restful bed;
he said his evening prayers—and drifted off.

* * * * * * * * * *

They sent his casket home; no bands nor fanfare there;
no gold star to display; no closure for the pain.
While politicians postured, he gave his country all;
his parents and his sweetheart mourned alone.

He sleeps beneath his Georgia clay—unsung.
It wasn't called a war—but he was called to die.

THE NEW DOMINION

Both nobly born and common man
from England crossed the sea,
and thus the Commonwealth began
with those who would be free

to spread themselves across the land
and settle where they could.
With hardships greater than they planned,
they still found freedom good.

From sturdy stock their leaders grew
with independent thought.
Protecting liberty, they knew,
could not be simply bought.

The price was high, but fully paid,
as brave men's blood was shed.
A nation then was loosely made;
Virginia's statesmen led.

The Commonwealth's diversity—
its greatest attribute,
with fishing from the bay and sea
and orchards filled with fruit.

The Shenandoah farms provide
fine food for rich and poor.
The massive rivers, long and wide,
link Blue Ridge to the shore.

The tempo of commercial North
contrasts with Southern pace.
The Eastern watermen go forth,
a wind-tossed sea to face.

A home for all who would be true
to those who paved the way,
the Old Dominion lives anew,
proud gem of USA.

MIKE MAGGIO

THE MASTER FITTER'S APPRENTICE

My master fitter,
I've seen your mannequins and pins, the way

a chestnut-stained fabric gently drapes your rigid
arm as you bend and crouch and kneel. Here

in this enchanted room, filled with wicked possibilities,
I've watched you measure and cut, envied the soft cloth

passing through your firm fingers, coveted the barren form's frigid
habit to welcome your tenuous touch. From this dark bitter

corner, where I gaze and await your command, I've furtively followed
the trace of your ring, now sparkling, now dull, a curious truce

between your secret eyes, resting briefly on my brazen shoulder,
and your heavy brow waxed by days and years of wonder and woe.

But for your bobbins, your buttons and lace
as wondrous as a Spanish galleon lost

underwater, crammed with gold and silver, muslin and aged tapestry,
I would ask: what of the smile that once graced your face,

the golden threads that wove the hushed yearnings bound beyond your distant
eyes. My master fitter, I will bring you bolts of cotton and silk, spools

of dappled velvet and sheer black satin. I will lay rolls of organza at your feet. I will
unfold the soft chiffon on your table and joyfully smooth it out for you

to render the silver stitches, the restive embroidery that conceals your ruthless charm.
Look: the moonlight stains your naked arm.

I feel a tremble rise up through your silken skin, and I fear
the wedding pleats are slowly ungathering

Iris of Spring

Iris of Spring,
you sprout luxurious
from your false bed of snow.

Enrobed in your splendid yellow and green,
so soft, so languid,
your willowy arms

outstretched,
your legs, concealed in a curious tangle,
your face, a wisp of woken wonder.

You unfold
quietly, tenderly,
tall and tempting

invite me to gaze, to touch
to linger
in your faint drowsy fragrance.

How came you to be like this?
What did you all winter
lying nestled in your frigid muddle of soil:

the earth, your covetous lover
the sun, feverish with want
the frost, a wicked reminder of your cruel absence.

Iris, I spy you couched in mystery
and yearn to seize you
long to capture your wondrous bloom

snatch you from your bold innocence
place you in a vase to adorn love's altar
to watch and wonder and adore.

Come now, let us not regret the future.
Let us revel in this brief moment.
Let us embrace this elusive season of bliss.

For Spring shall shed its silken sheen
Summer will rise,
then tumble into Fall

and I left here, alone,
as you surrender once again
to Winter's icy grip.

I shall await your resurrection.
Steadfast, I shall remain here,
agonized, canonized

as my longing, like the weeping stars,
endures the cold, bitter night.

JAMES IRVING MANN

CREATION IS CALLING.

The Glory of Creation
shines
in the rising sun
and in the blooming rose.

The Voice of Creation
speaks
in the thunder's roar
and in the sparrow's song.

The Beauty of Creation
thrives
in a redwood forest
and in a field of daisies.

The Presence of Creation
sings
in the winds of the desert
and in the howls of the wolf.

The Wonder of Creation
dwells
in snow-covered mountains
and in deep-ridge canyons.

The Joy of Creation
lives
in the birth of babies
and in the smiles of children.

The Silence of Creation
sleeps
in the glow of the moon
and in the gleam of the stars.

The Freedom of Creation
calls,
is calling us—
remember—
to share in creation.

Mike McDermott

Donut Trilogy

1

One AM. The "Hot Donuts NOW" sign is lit.
Cars pull across four lanes of Route 1 to fill the lot.
Pilgrims amble into the white-walled shrine,
sidle onto the low-slung stools,
and order a couple of hot glazed
from the back with a cuppa.
Old men, one or two, hunch over
empty coffee cups and stare with contempt
at newcomers. No soul.
Simply here for the donut with a center
one can see right through.

2

Like communicants who've come
to the rail for their daily bread,
men and women stand in line
for their ritual morning coffee
and, virtuously, one plain donut.

Or, maybe today, two
plain donuts, still virtuous
in their plainness, but
just this once, today,
two plain donuts.

Or, maybe, today,
just one with icing
and the other, of course,
even, sort of, good for you,
virtuously tastelessly plain.

Or, maybe, just today
one with icing, and one,
oh my goodness, only one
filled, yes, filled
with jelly, or chocolate,
or, oh my God, filled with cream.

Tomorrow, just one plain.

3

So much depends
upon

the golden round
donut

glazed with white
frosting

beside the hot
coffee.

Kindra McDonald

Could We Live?

This spring all the grocery stores have run
out of yeast. We are searching the aisles
for this single-cell organism, begging
our neighbors for flour, trying to track
down sourdough starters. We have all
been baking bread, and I break bread
virtually over computer communion
with the stale saltine I found in the cabinet
and dip into some cooking sherry, the sacrilege
of this sacred act.
We have all been baking bread;
it changes the smell of worry
in our homes to comfort. The melting
butter is like a pool of sun, filling
our stomachs with something
like love, but mostly when we knead
the dough, warm and living, soft
and pliant, it feels like hugging,
it feels like human touch.
If we could live on bread
alone; we could live on
bread that would somehow
make us whole, together alone.

Think of Such Things
   Philippians 4:8

Now trapped inside these four walls
lonely racing raindrops down glass panes
hands pressed to a past
my memory fogs like breath

Now when the home movies
of my life reel behind me
in Super 8 pastels of pink and blue
shadows dancing remember
how well the bathtub holds me
how the chair knows my shape
but can't contain me, when
I was water I curled and crashed
shocking cold and wild how I always
returned to the place I was born

When I was a tree I shook light
like golden tinsel, held up the shade,
drank in the rain, lifted the climbers
and each season shed and bloomed
grew again towards sky

When I was a bird I was a guide
to the fisherman, pointing out each
speckled scale, I knew rain was coming
by how my feathers tingled, when my
wings tired no matter how far I was
I knew just how to find home, building
nests from the bones of fish
The best of me mourns the salt spray
on my face, how my hair made a cape
behind me in the breeze, how the spider
climbs the spout not fearing rain
We are mirror selves, my best and me
When I was a child my heartbeat
was violins, my bare feet slapped
the gritty woody boardwalk immune
to splinters, skipping through surf
and spinning sand of praise and song

Open the door, put one foot in front
learn to run again even knowing I'll end
where sky meets sea—
this is faith to leap
becoming again and again and again

Anne Metcalf

The Egg

There is a specific way
To eat a soft-boiled egg
Perched in its little cup
With the hand-painted flowers
Tap the tip of the shell and
Gently lop off the top
Then plunge your spoon in to
Retrieve its molten contents

There is a specific way
To cook a soft-boiled egg
Fill the small pot halfway with water
Not more
Not less
Throw in a pinch of salt
Turn on the gas
(Be careful!)

When the water is boiling
Place the egg in the metal slotted spoon
And lower it into the water
Leave it in for
Four and a half minutes
Not more
Not less
(Remember to set a timer!)

While the egg is cooking
Take one piece of bread
Sourdough from the freezer
Place it in the toaster set on 4
Not more
Not less
Press down the lever
(Watch that it doesn't burn!)

When the timer goes off
Remove the egg from the water
With the metal slotted spoon
(Remember to use a mitt!)
Place the egg under a cold tap for fifteen seconds
Not more
Not less
To stop it from cooking further

Place the egg on a clean kitchen towel
Let it dry while you remove
The bread from the toaster
And cut it in half on the diagonal
And then once again
Not more
Not less
To make four triangles

Place a small pat of butter
On two pieces
Not more
Not less
Then place one atop the other to soften it
And the toast on the small white plate
The one without a chip
The one with the blue rim

Put the egg in the egg cup
The one with the tiny flowers
In the middle of the plate
On each of the toast triangles
Spread one half-spoonful of marmalade
Not more
Not less

Take a light blue quilted placemat—
An unstained one, the Christmas candles have leached red—
And a blue flowered napkin
From the top drawer
A calendar is stuck in the right hand corner
(Be careful when opening not to rip it!)

Place the placemat on the tray
Fold the napkin in half
Place it on the left
A knife and spoon on the right
Put the morning's pills in a small ramekin
Above the napkin

Fill a small glass
Halfway with juice
Not more
Not less
Place it above the spoon

(Remember how
Stemware is always on the right

Above the knives and spoons
From left to right
First the water
Then the Champagne
Then the wine?)

Place the plate
On the placemat
On the tray
Then carry it in

MY SWEDE

I've decided he is a Swede
And that we'll feast on
Boiled new potatoes
Slick with butter and dill
And salmon with *crème fraiche*
Flecked with caviar

We will laugh and sip
Cold pepper vodka
In small beveled glasses
And eye one another
From straight wooden chairs
Across a plain marble table

His hands are big
The skin speckled
On one he sports a black ring
The other a long white scar
Women often ask about
But I don't

I don't ask because
I don't need to know
I don't want to know
And even if I did
What would knowing
Really tell me?

I already know him
I know he stands and fights when tested
And that his father was mean
That sometimes his right knee gives out
So he knows not to run far
Or stray away from me

Alan Meyrowitz

Breaking

Pushing through
the crust of cooling custard,
no harm but that accepted
in the course of one's dessert

If only all my damage done
were so benign—
hearts were not so mindless
of their loss,
as cooling custard

Night Lilies

Shy by day, tightly furled,
heeding nightly call to bloom

How much the same,
my love demure till waning light,
so joy is sown in garden's bed
as well our own

Yet passion's not by season bound—
lilies will be gone by fall

Barbara Meyrowitz

Lonely

—in the time of COVID

If I can't see you
      I am blind

If I can't hear you
      I am deaf

If I can't touch you
      I am without feelings

If I can't kiss you
      I am without joy

I want to hold you
but I am here and
you are there

A Whisper Is

a sleeping baby's breath

a knowing glance

a flower blooming

a feather floating

a falling shadow

the line following this one

Heather Louise Morgan

I Saw Him Years Later

I saw him years later in a church in a suit
looking respectable from the neck down.

He leered at me,
"You grew up to be quite an attractive woman."

My new dress was stained by his eyes.
Ruined.

He held a little girl on his knee.
Every cell of my body screamed,

LEAVE HER ALONE!
But I said nothing.

A Salmon Pink Snow

A salmon pink snow
brightens the night.
Ice softens the city.

I'm blanketed
and long for warmth.
Where are you?

In a heavy house,
radiators run upstream.

An icicle falls from the eaves,
penetrates my woolen stillness.

Susan Notar

Botanica

My cottage lies at the village edge
roof masked in moss.
From the ceiling beams hangs mugwort
to promote dreaming and divination
bundles of rosemary
to banish burglars.

In morning young women arrive
seeking love and children.
For them I provide patchouli and basil oil
for sensuality
lavender for calm
and to quell their impatience.

To the old I proffer
sage smoke for wisdom
willow bark for aching knees
turmeric for inflammation or cancer.

In the late afternoon
Melancholia arrives
as she often does
particularly when the mist is thick.
To her I offer yarrow
to regain composure.

Night brings the fox.
See his glinting eyes
his burnt umber coat
as he sits by my hearth
tells me his exploits
before he vanishes
like the smoke from my chimney
talking to the trees.

Yezidi, Northern Iraq

A Yezidi woman sits across from me
her eyes flat black
like no eyes should look
as if her spirit has been sucked
backward through her body
to fly away somewhere else
somewhere safe
before
Kocho
Sinjar.

It is true?
her handler asks me
Is it true what ISIS did to the children?
She starts to cry
great rolling tears
streaking her face black mourning mascara.

I seek safety inside myself
in a world that offers none.

Is it true?
Is it true?

It is true.

I hear her voice
asking over and over
like the crows now cawing
over mass graves
as the Yezidi woman gazes
but not at me.

Michelle LT O'Hearn (Micki)

Creating a Green Scene
"Earth cares for her own ruins, naught for ours."
"The Burning of the Leaves," Laurence Binyon

Mother of the land: soil to sand
Objects borne, living, dead, absorbed.
Left behind to be composted, eaten, or reserved.
Once flesh stored in a box or jar as dust
with an emotional remnant of memory.
The child's tear, the spousal worry of debt,
the pain of loneliness with nowhere to rest bereft.
Nothing to digest that will dissipate screams.
Crying to Mother when Father ignores
no ears to hear and no response from the land.
Mother only to sand and we are not grit
lest we plant the brain in a reflection of it.

She smiles upon the tiniest green sprout,
hears no worry or doubt as all of her children
sing into the morning of the sun.
A droplet to moisten gently
plummeting at high-sky speed.
Touchdown absorbed with excess dripping
from the curve of the curled leaf and taken in
by thirsty dirt: a drink is shared.

We smile with delight at this loving interaction
and hope for a turn to play with more passion.
Yet she looks us over recurrent and again
never acknowledging our desire to be touched.
Impatient, we toss technology to the sky
in attempts to trigger a response,
only to feel disregarded and lost
when the reply she targets to the sea or glaciers.
We turn our craniums in forceful feign of satisfaction
to work on green salvation as a relentless distraction
from a single statement of truth:
Earth cares for her own ruins, naught for ours.

Winter Solace

Frosted ice on the window
foggy reflections in the glass
winter sparkles off the crystals
crispy footprints in the grass.

Warm hand upon the pane
melting eyes stare towards the road
hot car rolls across the pavement
fireplace hearth beats hard alone.

Colors flutter in the yard
feathers flying at the feeder
distracted eyes from inside
dry to smiles behind the heater.

Seeds flailing off the ledge
thrown down by bouncing feet
drifting to the snow below
into another ready beak.

Several minutes watching
mind drifts with the snowy birds
laughter rises without hesitation
as winter solace returns.

R. L. O'Kelly

The Lost Country

In a still moment
he said to himself,
he won't go again
into that country
where he first knew
oneness; then aloneness.
It is lost in smoke.
The heart can't find it now.
A little breeze of time
has disarrayed it.

He won't go again
into that country
to find the streets
his soul had foraged
for his dreams,
the bed his form
had long impressed;
the warmth of hands
that had clasped
his own hands.

He won't go again
into that country
to visit apple trees
under Northern stars
and stand before
the tomb of his father.
His kinsmen and women,
all lost in a mist,
tend those green gardens
the heart can't find again.

The Light in April

See them come.
Spokes of a wheel,
and the wheel turns

along a new track.
Freed from their sighing;
from the coughing,

their night full of winter
withdrawing behind them
dissipates like miasma, dream.

Now they find a way
through old oppressions
and many entanglements.

Their hands hold fast
to warming earth;
reach for newborn leaf.

Their eyes shine light
reflected from night
and turn toward the sun.

Nan Ottenritter

Tying the Bowline
For Michael who served, retired, then went to sea

he returns from days
on the open sea
tying bowlines
sharing 3 am watches

with nothing but a sea in sight
stars crowding out the night sky
waves raucous then silent
threads of hemp embedded in his hands

suddenly he is in port
duffle of dirty clothes in the trunk
hand on the radio dial
Afghanistan has fallen

his hand aches for the bowline
simplicity of focus
purpose and working hands
to soothe his breaking heart

Of Place
We are first in place, then of it.

1.

Germans are of place, she said. Yes, one may marry and move,
but once one locale is exchanged for another, we return to
miraculously clean windows, swept stoops, white lace curtains,
greenhouse tomatoes—all alive as yeast in the oven, embrace
in the bed. Flowers of red, purple perch on the sill,
cascade down uneven, medieval stone walls.

2.

In today's Before Time, we ploughed through the land,
noticed only when it scraped a shin or offered up a cool
sip of water from between moss-covered rocks,
a liquid gem amongst slippery mounds of danger.
Slowly, as the tree ringed itself and humus pressed,
we noticed a waft of green, song of the jay.

3.

Our Middle Time yard now blooms raised beds, compost with
egg shells and coffee grinds. We nourish newfound
progeny, protect them from aphids and cabbage worms,
water in the morning, visit at day's end, pull a weed, say
a prayer. We compliment our neighbor's squash, their new
puppy's romp. They sip our wine, share time.

4.

In quarantine we are more of place than ever. We walk
the neighborhood, searching the sameness for something more.
Kids tear up and down the streets on their bikes, little bands of
marauders pillaging difference. Our patio guests compliment
the crape myrtles, serenity of cut grass and potted plants.
We live in place, gently becoming of it as we await the After Time.

Little Lincoln

I haven't slept well.
The red neon sign at the breakfast dive blinks
Open. 6:50 a.m. The coffee's hot.

I shake the dust off my dreams; politics continue
to haunt. Stephen Colbert made me laugh,
tucked me in, then left me to my nightmares.

I ask my server how her pregnant co-worker is.
My sister? You mean the girl with the tattoos down her other arm?
My waitress's right arm, fully tatted, motions toward her plain left.

She's your sister? I didn't know that!
Yeah, she had the baby in August, calls him Lincoln.
Where'd she get the name Lincoln?

I think it's from Abraham Lincoln—she's a big history buff, reads a lot.
His middle name is Alyosha, or something like that. Can't pronounce it.
Her husband's from Iran. But I get to babysit and hold him on Sunday!

I sigh. If this young woman, working for minimum wage in a diner, one
semester short of a bachelor's degree, with her Iranian husband and several kids
in tow, names her newborn Lincoln Alyosha (or something like that) then all

will be well.

Marsha Owens

When the Osprey Return

wingspread casts a shadow
as he, clumsy acrobat
descends, drops to the pier
and touches down beside
her scratch-throated call,
a timeless taunt

two wings cover
two wings, rough
boards beneath them
dance this dance,
breezes bend the pine
branches

and i, reluctant witness,
glimpse nature
nudge itself forward
adorned in feathers,
while i, earthbound,
merely sense
the ancestral wind
that lures lovers

Boarded Up

windows
once framed faces
looking out, looking in,
pictures' eyes
hung on nails, watched life
shuffle across floorboards,
witnessed hands carry the strap,
or the scraps
for dogs under the porch.

Sundays dressed
in platitudes,
Crisco fried chicken
hand-printed on Grandma's apron,
Papa rocked after lunch,
his cigarette smoke
burned into mystery.

Boarded up now, the house
slumps into silence
mired in muddy
tracks in the yard,
conversations carried off by rats,
chickens gone.

Hurricanes

I've thought little today about the pandemic stomping around everywhere,
focused instead on Hurricane Isaias that passed through Virginia near my house
on the Chesapeake Bay in yesterday's early morning hours, but today, coffee cup
in hand, I welcome the sun, watch the feisty hummingbird chase his competitor
from the feeder, and I'm reminded of the cliché, *life goes on*, though here at the
river I worry about leaky windows from the last nor'easter, from storms that
startle without warning, wind that whips around this small patch of land where
our tiny white cabin sat safely for years, built from rough-hewn boards by a
white man and a black man working side by side, sharing mutual respect one
for the other, my Daddy and Pete, the man who lived on the island. Outside the
cabin one day, I saw Pete tip his hat to my mother—and to me—a five-year-old
child because in the 1950's South, people who may have wished things were
different understood they were not, Pete knew his place, and I, I knew nothing
about race or civil war or hangings, hate or hurricanes, so I tucked myself
behind Mama's apron, not knowing that day would be one of our last days
together, that this would be the last summer she'd be with us at the river, but I
remember clearly what she said… *Thanks for your help, Pete*, as she handed him
a plate with a hot dog and baked beans she had warmed up on the one burner
stove, that he ate on the stoop outside our kitchen door.

Linda Kennedy Partee

A Capitol Affair

Performing briefly every spring, we watch
unfurling costumes shaken loose and plumped,
appearing silently all powdered pink
until they fill the stage with quiet grace
to dip and sway to secret melodies,
like Geishas trained for entertainment's joys.

Endearments sweetly whispered fill the air
like butterfly flirtations, velvet-veiled
to kiss their minions' cheeks with innocence—
a barely-there confetti silk caress.
Embraced and smitten, wrapped in beauty's spell,
admirers play their part in nature's scene.

Without an audience, would dancers bow
or twirl and rustle clustered coronets;
would smooth enchanters scatter carefree charms,
and ballerinas toss kimonos free?
One blink, quick wink before the magic fades,
when cherry blossoms crown a nation's throne.

Salem Soliloquy
Massachusetts, 1692

Devils wearin' church face, church face, church face
devils with their church mask on.
Devils wearin' church face, church face, church face
devils with their church mask on.

Hee-hee, hi-hi, ho-ho, hum,
look out, Salem, here they come—
wearin' pious faces, sayin' prayers on end,
holdin' far-fetched suspicion of a neighbor or a friend.
Accusers are the young girls barkin' like the dog,
spewin' curses from their lips, croakin' like a frog.

Devils wearin' church face, church face, church face
devils with their church mask on.

First, have the doctor examine and conclude,
"Gotta handful of witchcraft startin' up a feud."
Behavin' so peculiar, instillin' fear in most,
showin' all the townfolk Satan is their host.
Pointin' skinny fingers, doomin' elders straight to hell,
blamin' them for the curse of their black magic spell.

Devils wearin' church face, church face, church face
devils with their church mask on.

Superstitious gossip is the wick that fuels your mess,
as more and more innocents are forced to confess.
Startin' in the morning into winter's early night,
gallows hang the guiltless because of your own fright.
God forgive you Salem, better drop to your knees
and beg His pardon for these necks that you squeeze.

Devils wearin' church face, church face, church face
devils with their church mask on.

Hee-hee, hi-hi, ho-ho, hum,
look out Salem, here they come—
powerless young maidens still cravin' bright light
will spread their lies all dressed in white.
Tight-collared clergy and frock-coated jury
damn those accused in quite a big hurry.
In spite of the evidence, defined by men,
twenty unjust murders did happen then.
	Amen, brother, amen.

Devils wearin' church face, church face, church face,
devils with their church mask on.
Devils wearin' church face, church face, church face,
devils with their church mask on.

Christian Vincent Pascale

Gypsum Dunes

The Martian walks on gypsum dunes.
He is the last one of his kind.
Once wet and warm, now left in ruins,
Mars so resembles Earth's cold moon.

Three billion years, or more, ago
The airboats flew cross crystal seas
And through the wetlands rivers flowed.
The loss of atmosphere the key

To disappearance of the seas.
Hesperian age came to an end.
The solar winds caused air to flee.
Then to Earth's womb her life would send

On rocket wings the cargo flew.
Archean Age when life began.
From death of one the other grew,
Five million years the rise of man.

The Martian walks on gypsum sand
Remembers breeze on summer seas
In dreams returns to former land's
Forgotten images of trees.

Ghosts at the Table

I thought that more people would have mourned.
Certainly from our church,
the church he had left to stand for a principle
they no longer considered valid, but sacred to him.

My wife and I revisited his favorite restaurant,
the site of many former after-church lunches
with him and his wife; just the four of us
talking about kids and grandkids. He loved my son deeply.

My wife and I sat in silence thinking about the two empty chairs
across from us at our table, once filled with joy.
The waitress asked about them.
They were her friends, treated her like a daughter.

I saw her wipe the tears from her face when I told her why
he and his wife no longer came.
I had to avert my eyes. My wife started to cry as well.
And so, in silence, we ate with ghosts.

The manager came to our table, his pain evident.
The waitress had told him, and he wanted to say how sorry;
"They were really good people," he said. "I hope she is okay."
He wanted to know details, and I told him what I could.

His wife would get through this, I said. She is with her daughter.
But I did not know if I would. Get through it, that is.
I thought of the years of service he had given our church.
Now, he was mourned by me, my wife, a waitress, and a manager.

The others might write their letters, which his wife did not want to read.
I would not write. I had spoken to her. We would speak again.
So I sat at the table and thought what he would say if he were there.
The memories ached. It was just me, my wife, and the ghosts at the table.

HER ROOM UPSTAIRS

Your clothes are on the bed upstairs
Your bright red dress and underwear
Laid out as for some grand event.

The room arranged just like a shrine
To memories of what was mine,
Just like the roses that I sent.

So faded now, just lost somehow
Like laughter and our wedding vows,
The promised years that we once spent.

This spring I will unlock the door,
Let in fresh air and sweep the floor.
And fix our bed that now is bent.

Perhaps fresh flowers from our yard
Will somehow fix the room that's marred
By stale perfume's intrusive scent.

But if I took that scent away
Your memory might never stay.
I'd live a life of discontent.

I think I'll leave things like they are.
For one should never go too far
Removing love's long lost lament.

Steven P. Pody

East Virginia

In the loving arms of rivers, East Virginia's lands unfold.
From the Blue Ridge to the ocean,
a most magnificent tale is told.
We may catalogue her virtues, nature blessed each verdant mile;
you may rush along her trail ways,
or kick back and pause a while....
North, along a pretty valley, and to the south runs too,
the lifeblood of Virginia,
found in story, song (and view!)
The James and Shenandoah,
tumble-flow to bay and sea.
Appomattox and Rappahannock,
likewise course through history.
Respect to Chief Powhatan, the first Virginian named,
though he knew of no such boundaries,
still, he's fated to be thus famed.
At future Jamestown, new dreams landed,
three ships presaging bold migration,
melding local and fresh-quest destiny,
as blended culture; mighty nation.
But beyond old native spirit, and colonial overlay.
Beyond uncivil battles; blood and tears that soaked the clay.

Surpassing shackle, and imperfect triumph, with

men and women, heads unbowed,
panoramic Ol' Virginny
lies lovely, bountiful and proud.
As cascading waters turn eastward,
and calm to sluggish flow;
and likewise, high Appalachia
levels east, as fields to sow;
and the easterly sea...gifts vistas,
on the abundant Virginian shore,
they round out vast variety that each person should explore.
The glories of a remarkable State,
endow grandeur for hand and heart;
bestows delight to every eye,
and sets Virginia
quite apart.

On Wings of Dappled Clarity

Hush….
   …Hardly comes the might to whisper
or speak of subtle, wondrous things,
when I am inclined to silent muse,
that gives my heart
                    its glimmer'd wings.
The challenge is…to listen.
Perhaps intent in a raw city night….
A pulsing potential
                    'neath darkened veil,
or contemplative in meadow'd sunlight.
Wings upon the wildflowers!
Appreciatively I sit, with near-grasp.
Bounty, Gaia herself
                    has fashioned,
and worthy souls seek to enclasp.
…Then, to serenity's loom, compound senses;
more consciousness imbuing the stream.
A blush of music fills my eyes,
with nary discord to the theme.
I taste the stars,
                    and feel their dance;
comprehend the mountain's scent.
And, in the amber lilt of dusk,
I empathize…what was meant.
I sing on the wings of the cosmos;
fathom seas of bless'd habitat.
Refreshed, I am ever-astonished!
      True beauty
                    is much like that….

Trilla Ramage

The Handkerchief

After you died,
after your handsome frame
and silver curls became ashes

After the final accounting
closed the book on a lifetime of hard work;
after the recounting
of the acts of humanity, frailty and courage

After

My brother, reigning patriarch,
gently gave out the only tangible connection
left to possess: your handkerchiefs.

14 x 14 white squares,
meticulously pristine, creased in half,
then quartered, halved twice more.

Clean, durable cotton
—untouched by starch—
ready to dry the brow
or to wipe a child's nose.

At hand to collect
the unfolding of each day
whether borne of honest work,
an outburst of laughter or
the occasional heartbreak.

Our first lesson
of ironing, folded and pressed,
becomes your last gift:

soothing,
absorbing these tears
as the measure and the treasure
of this day,
                    this father.

Thimble Memories

My mother occasionally gathered her daughters
and drove Route 23 to their world's very edge.
An uninspired storefront teetered there in neglect.
Oh, but its sign boasted audacious goods: Buttons and Bows.
A seamstress extraordinaire, mother's creations
often carried a flare of whimsy adorned with the unexpected:
navy ducks, white stars, yellow daisies, bas-relief metals.

Unlike my sisters, the sewing gene skipped my DNA.
Begrudgingly, I can resew a button or snap,
thread a machine and guide its needle for straight hems.
Even so, the magic of store's aisles left me breathless
from its array of colors, fancifulness, sizes, materials, forms.

With the stealth and determination only a child possesses
my hunt was not for the cavernous space's namesakes.
I had eyes only for the random jars gleaming with beads,
glass and porcelain masterpieces of jeweled exquisiteness.
Possessed by awe and magic, I'd tumble beads, endlessly
marveling at the minute artistry, mesmerizing luster and
myriad imagination: balls of flower chains, lurid stripes
and miniature animals. I swayed to siren songs of faraway
lands and peoples of enchantment.

It takes but a thimble to make me remember
those trips across seas on imagined clipper ships
launched from the edge of my world on Route 23.

Richard L. Rose

Inhale
Song from *Tales Since the Shift*

Just take one breath
on this side of forever.
Embrace all gifts.
Hold joy and grief together.
Hold, gladly welcome
all of life and death.
Just take one breath.

Just give one breath.
In formless darkness diving,
embrace all gifts.
Emptied of tasks and striving,
give, keeping nothing.
Cleansed, begin again.
Just give one breath.

We share the breath
of all awake and sleeping.
Their breaths we hold
like treasures in our keeping.
In all the flying, running,
crawling, creeping;
in every leaf and fungal thread
all share one breath.

LIFT OFF
In memoriam. SBR

Exhale.
Set meters to aught.
Let sorrows depart.
Exhale.

Let go.
Instruments, zero.
Forget what you know.
Let go.

Pierce eyes.
Fly with your heart.
Let sorrows depart.
Pierce eyes.

Anne H. Roseman

Backyard Philosophy
"The sleep of reason produces monsters." Francisco Goya

Late afternoon is a time I often sit
Outside to observe my bamboo forest
Knowing deep down the roots reach out
Connecting in a cross-stitched pattern
Like the quilt covering me.
A wind picks up and I wonder—was this in the
Weather forecast for today? I wonder, too, what
Is that sound from the bamboo forest? It is more
Than just the wind. Listen: "hoo-hoo'to-hoo-ooo."
Three times I hear this and then, flying from the
Bamboo forest, straight toward me in my chair are
Three owls. Yes, my family, my owl family, and I
Think that this is finally my time.

Sea Foam

Fierce waves pound the sand and push up,
Up to sift through sea grass, pushing even
Farther up, landing with a loud roar mingling
With the wind, it too, roaring, swirling foam
Like bath bubbles over the road bringing with it
Seaweed mixed with plastic bits—bottle caps,
Condoms, and paper cups from beachcombers
Who left their sand oasis just minutes before
Not wanting to be caught with the fierce waves' undertow.

DAVID ANTHONY SAM

THE RELATIVE BENDING OF TIME

The spring equinox
does not pause....

The slant of planet,
the revolution of it
around a sun and the ellipse
of its orbit combine
to bring alteration to
the state of water,
to the state of minds
that begin to unburden
themselves from caverns
carved in blue snow.

Does this signify time?
Is time in the breaking
of solid rivers into
a tinkling of brash ice?
Is time in the warmth
that melts life green?

I find the time
to stand against the slant
of sun across the freed
lake, shimmering in waves.

I find the time
to measure my heartbeats
and my breathing against
the lap of wave to shore.

I find the time is green
and understand a year
by seasons. But, really,
the divisions are of the mind.

There is no day when time
stops for a moment
and waits to cross
some imaginary
line. There is no moment
when ice becomes green.

There is no time
but a bending of space
in the ice that decorates
my hair and eyes.

And yet, somehow,
there is a spring.

The Invention of Zero

The calendar of earth
pages ultimate days
towards absolutes of zero.
Final ice will glaze
in brittle slivers
like bits of bone.

> The vulture that flies the vacuum
> has the voice
> of silence
> in its dark migration.

A nebula is the original garden.
It flowered stars—
the holy unnamed waiting
for the namer
who betrayed meaning
in the naming of the parts.

> Do you succumb to sunsets
> in their eerie stumbling light
> measureless as silent flights
> of white-nosed bats
> tumbling towards extinction?
> They sing above our register
> as they feed on dark flights,
> rendering the black sky
> with dying ink.

The clock of the sun
writes the red hours
in boiling eyes.
I dare not look away
from the final blindness.

The egg has broken open
and the Perseids of incomplete worlds
fall in arcs of missiles.

Track the dying in red footprints
written in whiteness of snow
as the augury of prime numbers.

The sacrilege of my blue fingers
mocks the zero
that must follow.

J. C. Scott

Fluidity

Like a drop of rain, I am gloriously fluid
Like an aging bloom, I am delicately human
Like a surf worn rock, I am smoothly hardened
Like an innocent child, I possess feelings of love
Like a worried parent, I am constantly thinking
About the reasons, I live perpetually alone

There are those who may say, it is best to be alone
when definitions allude, and set genders are fluid
Motivations questioned, life's untrusted thinking
Though emptiness is death, and solitude never human
Is it not pre-destined for all to seek out love?
Is it not avoidable for us to become so hardened?

Hearts are best left open, not closed off and hardened
At one time him, at one time her, but never alone
Do I not deserve to find my one true and final love?
Am I to be erased from life for such a curse of being fluid?
Straight or winding, narrow roads, I, a devoted human
of an oft deconstructed community, by my way of thinking

When did it transition back, this hatred infused thinking?
When "those" people push, hearts become hardened
No punch-drunk shades of gray when it comes to being human
Standing on a crowded street corner, devastatingly alone
The blood running cold, the heart skipping, erratically fluid
as passersby hold hands, unconsciously mockingly in love

For what does traditional mean exactly when one is in love?
Those feelings, deep as the Mariana Trench, it's my thinking
that time may pass us by, sand dropping, constant and fluid
but those feelings, the only constant, battle tested and hardened
as the last best defense, against a soul out of body and alone
Such notions become exquisitely genderless, but uniquely human

Is it not desirable to be one such perfectly imperfect human
that is acceptably capable of choosing the terms of love?
Or is it not only forbidden, but then too sequestered alone
in a book's deceptively parsed phrases, devoid of rational thinking
by phony cisgender hypocrites, so pretentiously hardened,
mistakenly trading on fashion as the definition of fluid

So, I stand, nakedly human, war torn and thinking,
like a migrant seeking hope in lands not yet hardened,
still ingloriously alone, still gloriously fluid

UPRIVER

Every day is a war-torn struggle within the mind's eye
Every second is a mind's eye view of malaria-like thoughts
Every paddle up stream on the river of certain return
Makes the salmon-like realization of one's divergence worth living
Is that so?

I was born upriver, so was already confused when identity came knocking
Messy molecules of cold sweat dripping like rainbow ice cream in Key West
My heart was closed-up and protected like a Fort Knox box full of love
He/him, she/her, they/them, and all I had to whisper was a sonic boom YES!
Who never looked so good?

A dash of fashion and a passion for fishing, and all essential ingredients
For the perfect recipe in the bestselling cookbook of confusion supreme
Choose carefully, which lane on the gendered highway, toll booth ahead
Rejection from the six-sided grandstander, careening off transition's onramp
Why can't you quantify it?

Downstream, upstream, or maybe the slipstream, any which way to flow
One is easy and one is hard, but the only true blue-ribbon is choice *du jour*
Alone at Garbo's table, waiting on destiny's menu to be hand delivered
I would at least have thought one could get a decent martini in this joint
Will there be anything else?

Well, that was certainly a *here's your hat what's your hurry* kind of moment
Maybe there's no saferoom as advertised, in this violently terse stream at all
One simply wants a blissfully symbolic kiss, and another wants a whole lot more
Which to choose and what to give, relenting realizations of a rippling reflection
Who gave you my name again?

Leslie Sinclair

War Story

While grown-ups fought, elected leaders tried
to send their children far away from fear.
Your Granny didn't write this down; we pried
it from long-buried depths; so, listen, dear:

"Those aunties in the country wouldn't see
as Mummy saw; she brought us back to war,
where bombers flew to airplane factory,
and dumped their excess payloads at our door.

One night—with sirens wailing—breaking sleep,
we scrambled out to shelter underground.
An earthquake, from no fault-line, thundered deep
so close that Mummy blanched: 'That's our house, downed.'

Not ours—but opposite, the rubble lay.
It buried Dave and drove his kin away."

Kathy Smaltz

Gypsy Woman

She was a sort-of gypsy, my mom,
wore broom skirts and bangles
on her wrists, waist-length hair
splayed out as she spun.

With her, I learned to sing
into one end of a jump rope,
Stevie Nicks's throaty voice
a melodic undercurrent.

There were other nights though,
when she'd go out to dance, pause
for a drink, wipe one palm, face down
on the smooth polish of the bar.

On those nights, I sang by myself,
played her *Rumors* album, the one
with pony-tailed Mick bending down
to hold Stevie's hand, both of them
young and beautiful.

She wanders the universe now,
knows more than she did before.

I see her riding the tail of a comet,
young and beautiful again
her skirt ballooning out, her bracelets
bangling, her hair splayed out behind her,
singing with me again, somehow,
for all the times I sang alone.

Roosevelt Lake

Quiet on the lake
this morning, marshy grasses
thick at its shore where water laps
against the weed-choked bank.

Sycamores seek sun at 45-degree
angles, stretch out to the blue-grey
shallows where the wind dances with
the sun's reflection, a mad mirage in scherzo.

A woodcock calls, perched in pine
on alert for fish not far
from the lines where we cast:
our orange bobbers float
while we too watch and wait.

Barbara Drucker Smith

Snoopy

Snoopy a ball of white fluff
Came home in a shoe box
With room to spare—fourteen years ago
West Highland Terrier, downward
       crooked tail
Ears pointing up, pink on the inside
Two years old followed Lisa to the
       pool
Did synchronized underwater turns as she did,
Up for air when she breathed. A showman,
Snoopy stepped up his pace
When the Black Lab, leash in mouth, walked him,

Rode ocean waves on float to shore
Barked in enclosed run...
More content on a clothesline
Sniffed, played with wandering dogs.
Held near my face,
Licked and licked my eyes, my cheek...
I whispered, "Good doggie, good stuff, my doggie"
Wrestled six-month-old Lab
Jumping, sniffing, licking, biting,
Size no obstacle,

Brown eyes slowly covered
With cataracts turning eyes blueish,
Vet put him under
To x-ray before leg operation,
Machine broke. Snoopy came home,
Overcame lameness naturally,
Touch of arthritis—never operated
Somewhat incontinent—needed regular outings
Spring, energetic, sniffing
Staking out his territory—urinating, running, urinating.

Vet called after I arrived back from Israel.
Snoopy died a week earlier of old age,
Probably a heart attack,
Seemed perfectly okay before he died
So the vet said,
Cremated Snoopy—hoped I didn't mind.

Unearth the Dusty Smell of Memories

Unearth the dusty smell of
Muck, mire, sulphuric, encrusted rocks
Oozing mud, between my toes
Mud covered my body at the Dead Sea
Brine, eye stinging, pungent

Desert sand of Nevada
Archeological digs in Jerusalem
Mountain top towns of Portugal and Spain
Tibetan dirt road fifteen hundred feet above sea level

Nagashima volcanic eruptions
Cause cars to stay dusty
That finger drawing shows up on cars' surfaces

Dirt roads of Maui, Hawaii
En route to pineapple plantations

Mule trail going from rim of Grand Canyon
To Yellow River at the bottom
Mule hide blocks my vision going down

All of the above including
The camel walking near the
Pyramid in Egypt
Unearth the smell of memories

Ron Smith

Declaiming

When my father takes my poems
in his fight-broken hands,
he holds my few words
at arm's length,
raises his rich, unused voice,
and calls each syllable
so carefully you can see
him declaiming Bryant
fifty years ago, at attention
beside his lunch pail
in the single room of Stilson School.

There, his cheeks are full of blood,
and he is handsome.
Parris Island is two years north.
He smells like the cows he milked
in the early Georgia dark.
He moves down each row
of phrases with the grimness
of those who feel
they must make the earth yield
its sweet corn,
its crouching Japanese,
catching up against
hard roots, going on

up the burning islands of the Pacific,
peering into the flaring dark
of each step north.
Against beachhead sunsets he sees
the Zeros sputter and go down.
In foxhole after foxhole he dreams
of dusty fields where he falls
behind the mule
and the rows close over him
and he comes up changed,
atabrine yellow,
wavering in the merest breeze,
his body whispering.

The days have gathered
into straight lines behind him.
After half a century
of the silent heft of steel
he is left with a handful
of somebody else's words,
words that slip
between thick, crooked fingers
like the lightest of seeds.

Its Ghostly Workshop

(advice to my grandson Russell Byrd Whistle Chad Smith)

Remember the memorable and let the rest go.
Of course, some part of everything is memorable.
Savor the detail and the barbarous language
it insists on speaking. Befriend all words.
Never fail to eavesdrop on the exotic
or the eternal. Force conversation with
the transient. Son, you can always
spare a dime.
                    Every now and then
empty what we are pleased to call
your mind. Let a cool wind blow through,
seal it with solitude, open it
to featureless horizons. Yes,
a Roman cistern or flat ocean
where no one, not even you,
exists. A long walk on an abandoned
railroad track can do the trick. It goes
without saying you must keep your mouth
shut and always go alone. Call it
meditation, if you like.
                    Entertainment?
Never mindless entertainment, a form
of desperation, highly addictive.
Let all your entertainment be mindful.
Monitor cumulus crossing the blue,
now Australia to Iceland, now Rushmore
to Matterhorn. Study the sky a little each day.
And, yes, often at night, but ignoring
constellations, if you can, making your own
and sweeping them away like sand painting.
Better star and stark nothing than centaurs
and lyres.
            Never take the image of a thing
for the thing, photo for face, landscape
for the land. Remember always that
perception is more than half creation,
the mind's no projection screen, transforms
what it receives, shuffles what's transformed,
makes of sunlight and synapse what the eye
has no rod, no cone to encounter.
That plain vision is visionary.

                              "Too much
time on your hands" is the mantra of
the miserable. Shun such judges. Kill clichés
in their cradles. They grow to monsters.
Let others think outside the box they have
hammered for themselves. Build no box
to begin with. Know what everyone knows
is not knowledge but preference of belief,
no more the truth than the shade is the shade tree.
Observe how abstractions self-assemble
to frame and shingle what the frightened head
thinks it needs for shelter.
                              Have faith in the truth
and its hermitage, its ghostly workshop.
Close your mind like a hand on the handle
of each handy fact, but never forget
an occupied hand can't grasp the new.
Don't wield too long nor grip too hard
what you take for truth. Be always prepared
to let it go. Let it go.

ELIZABETH SPENCER SPRAGINS

SONGS OF THE SOUTHERN RIM
Grand Canyon Village, Arizona

Quiet calls
From the corners of these walls
As a frosted sun descends
And lends flame to painted halls.

Raven wings
Whisper when the canyon sings
Lullabies of lavender
On her harp of piñon strings—

Grace note soars!
Condors row on silent oars,
Ferry cargo of my dreams
Over streams to heaven's shores

As dusk falls.
One last breath—the warm wind stalls
Just before the daylight dies.
Red rock sighs and quiet calls.

WHAT TREES REMEMBER
Chatham Manor, Fredericksburg, Virginia

Knotted knees
Bend beneath the memories
Of so many guns and groans.
Stones that ring catalpa trees

Do not speak
Of shattered bones, strong men weak
With fever, fear, and despair.
No prayer strokes the bloodied cheek

Of the dead.
Horses, hounds, and flocks have fled.
No one tills the trampled clay—
Torched plantations yield no bread.

The fall breeze
Blankets earth with rusted seas.
Colors of the dawn unfold,
Kiss the cold from knotted knees.

Sofia M. Starnes

Why Honeymoons are Brief

Although the evening light outflames their room,
although it skims their shadows on the rug
(a rug of Indian oceans and tall reeds),
and warms the woolen hollows—

And though they lie on skeins and stare up high,
as if the spackled ceiling were the dusk,
and underneath, a calendar of streets,
a temporal bemusement—

Although the finished spread seems nothing
but the burgeoning of tender, tender touch,
they learn what we once learned:
there's nowhere far.

A restless voice cries out across the street
and steals what twilight gives them, tipping earth;
the dual scents of lamb and mint converse,
and mindless of the door, feasts wander in.

No matter if they pull the shades, latch inwardly
the locks; the world must sneak its aches, its carbon in.
Won't one of them respond: cheeks risen, feverish?
And won't the other pray with human breath?

THE SOUL'S LANDSCAPE

Ah, what the soul gives for shape—
        to be handled head-first

at the temple, to be cumbered with cotton,
        white puffs from plantations

in heat; what it gives, for the flick, flick
        elastic on wrists, loose-leaf palms it

befriends, at its youngest—
        for the sake of all this, and this place.

Love me now with your hands (says the soul,
        half-exploring its landscape),

better me with embodiment; come,
        angle the ribs where they beach into

longing; come, finger the oval description
        of death, smallest hope for cessation.

When the room is redundant of space,
        and its walls wish for closure, thumb

my corners up, inward, wade your lips
        through the ridge where they meet,

to allow recollection.
        I must love with the tissue and the gloss

that embody: cellule, elegy, ghost, danger,
        languish...

all those words out of context for souls, god-
        forsaken, whiplash of the neck—

                        Interim,
that's the word I would use the most

cautiously; how precarious its hum, ear
        to earth, plumbing earth, earth-wise.

Baptism of Desire

By way of longing, winter has its eye
on red wings negotiating timber limbs,
blood-rose and tailwind from the winter
bird: and nowhere nests, and nowhere

rest for saints. This I would see and call it
my concern. But only if I'd cradled her;
her feathers tufting, eager to be spared—
and nowhere nest, and nowhere rest

for beasts. Apocalyptic is too long a sigh,
the evening light translates to evening
wind. Again, an eye on whirled and wintered
bird. Awareness is the proper name for nest.

Restless we live; a penknife scrapes a ply-
wood, hinges harp; thud is the shutter's
grim reminder that it shakes. The world's alert
to feelings and to flukes. Until, confessed,

we hunger for the birds.

Joyce Carr Stedelbauer

In the Beginning...

BEFORE silvery planets tumbled into space like dice
or stars light the way or moons pull tides,
time knew no memory, longing or forgiving,
color was squeezed into little paint tubes.

Fiery red—too hot to touch, blue cool enough for dawn,
yellow strong to stand in Van Gogh's haystacks,
purple hidden in mollusk shells, and elusive
green, so difficult to capture on canvas.

BEFORE wind and rain and heat grew into atmosphere
or water roiled and played together like laughter without
any salty tears or schools for fish
or ravens said nevermore or doves made peace.
Capricious sun chased rainbows over mountains boulders
split and slid into valleys,
pebbles skipped into the sea and cocoons released
brilliant butterflies like painted silk air.

BEFORE gazelles could leap or lions roar,
even before elephants could remember,
breezes eased into breathing and wind chimes
played lullabies, trees often waved hello,
snowdrops, sunflowers and night blooming jasmine
sweetened the air, and lovers always whispered goodnight.

Angel choirs sang "Alleluia"
in the beginning,
GOD.

Jamestown Musings

What if I had touched my toes on this New World seashore
after four months of heart thudding waves—
my hopes rising and falling on endless water
and the mood of the sky?
The clouds rolled back, opening windows of blue.
An anemic sun washed the sand.
I gasped for air sweetened with honeysuckle.
The trees so tall they swept memory of mist-iced
winging ropes, creaking wood, slippery decks,
monotonous food, frightful sanitation.
What if I had a hungry infant searching
for strength I did not have to give?
Finally, ashore, we are assigned a hut
vacated by death, the pioneer couple
succumbed to the sorrows of their first winter.
Early in the mornings the women tied up
their skirts and hair in favor of hoes and rakes
before the swelling sun sucked us dry.
Then the boiled laundry was ready to be hung,
swinging like pale ghosts of yesterday,
on ropes strung between the trees.
An iron pot of broth swung over a voracious fire,
eating sticks gathered by skinny children.
I pared the vegetables today, potatoes
onions, carrots, a few precious beans.
Would I have been allowed
to paint a forest scene or write a journal,
sew a pinafore or doze on my sagging cot
in the sticky heat of afternoon?
Books were as rare as a piano, so I learned
to make up stories to tell at bedtime,
listen for the music of hundreds of birds,
black wings, golden beaks, crimson feathers
flashing among dove grays, blues, and browns.
When the precious spools of thread were exhausted
we waited months for new supplies
on the next ship from home, fabric too, as prized as silver,
bolts of patterns and prints carefully measured as time.
For there was always soap to be made, perfumed
with plant oils, tallow dipped on long white wicks,
preserves boiled from berries gathered in the woods,
or bark stripped from logs for the next buildings.

I always looked forward to Sunday's worship hour
sitting under the thatched roof of the chapel,
listening for rain as soft as my pillowed tears.
Sometimes I spoke to the Vicar about my longing for England.
He told me to forget all that, this is the New World.
So every evening we lit candles in the gathering darkness,
shared our meager meal around a table spread with love,
bowed our heads to thank our Maker,
knowing all too well, we needed Divine protection
to survive another day.

ERICA STEPHENS

THE ROSE OF HOPE

Hope found itself within the crystal blue waters of Honolulu
and traced itself back to the mainland of America
where she weathered the bedrock for citizens,
natural born and immigrant, to rise

In the land of America, a dream is not only a dream but,
it is a message of manifestation from within,
pushing for the betterment of one's kind,
despite darkness, trials, and tribulations,
from one's past, present, and future

It is the captured vision of success
eaten halfway off silver plates of white-collar workers
I serve in the evenings,
that push me to go beyond what I might currently be,
for something,
for someone,
greater

and so I reach
stretching further than
the second-class citizen goals society set for me
focusing keenly on the prize like bald eagles
locking in on their prey,
a persistence praised yet envied from afar

Who is America at his worst?

Who is America at his best?

We are persistent, dependable
mustard seeds found within the lifeless, dank straw of a haystack:
persistent we conquer,
to mold new foundations,
to conquer greatness and set new standards,
to thrive for generations,
to represent diverse populations,
who will reach beyond those generations we see today.

We are the people,
but hope is only found where the people roam together

Where is the hope that lay upon the surface of crystal blue waters,
surrounded by blue jade vine and the smell of nectar
off the bank of the Promised Land?

How did our rose of hope stem,
when she grew up from concrete
dreaming to be as blessed as you,
as blessed as me,
as blessed as we,
in America

THE 'BACCA FIELD

Last night, I retraced the steps
of my ancestors' blood. I put
one foot in front of the other,
dug one hand in wet terrain,
and screamed to God under
a dark moonlight. I prayed
my deepest prayer and
realized that the 'bacca field
belonged to me, to my ancestors.
It belonged to every Black woman
and man who tended to crops
tenaciously 'til their hands calloused
and bled three times more than expected.

Last night, I retraced the steps
of my ancestors' blood. I felt my ancestors
speak to me through finely divided
'bacca lines. I heard them: "Run,
my child. Run. Run. Run." I put one foot
in front of the other and felt Earth
open beneath me. I retraced
the steps of my mother,
of my grandmother, of my grandfather,
of a lineage who dripped gallons of blood
in 'bacca fields, just so I could be
living proof that the legacy still reigns.

Dancing with Deer

We rise—pitch-black night,
whose only light,
translucent Hunter's Moon
and blanket of stars
F L U N G across autumn sky.
We come to the quiet meadow
in early morning hours,
set our folding chairs alongside river
in mountain's moon-shadow.

It is so still—so cold—there are no words—
the only sound, an unbroken chuckle—
water burbling over rocks, chasing itself downstream.
We await the deer and dawn.

We rise, open car windows,
allow new sounds to merge with night:
cello's rich dark molasses spills out—
violin and bass embroider the edges.
"Appalachian Waltz" floods the darkness—
sounds magnified by silent hills.

Grateful for warmth, we move into each other's arms.
'Round and 'round we turn,
letting the night music fill us,
while in the darkened meadow,
('though we cannot see them—
shy creatures that they are)
we know the deer, too,
are dancing.

WISHFUL THINKING

My eighty-year-old mother
rests in the truck's cab at a red light,
contentedly licking an ice cream cone,
grandson at the wheel.

Her walker is stowed in back.
There is chocolate on her chin
as they sit the crosswalk,
companionable silence spanning generations.

Two young women
step off the curb,
begin an undulating stroll.
My mother leans forward, all interest.

Bright red and purple,
their revealing mini-skirts cling,
gold earrings dangle—
high, high heels on strong tanned legs.
They laugh and toss their heads in passing.

Silence lengthens in the truck, ice cream forgotten.
The light changes; they move forward.
My mother turns to her grandson,
smiles, says with deep satisfaction,

"I used to look like that."

Caren Stuart

I Am Not Spew Marrow Creek

I am not Spew Marrow Creek.
I am not the tributary born of the bubbling up spot
of the spring at the iron stake where the woods
meet the brambles.
I am not the split streams fanning out
through the cow fields,
welling up in marshy lowlands,
sinking Harry Davis Road.
I am not the runnel, the rindel, the rill
making mad, muddy way through
gully, ditch, or trough.
I am not contained by these reedy bogs,
these rip-rapped shores, these rock-riddled cliffs.
I am not constrained, not charted.
I am droplets tumbling through leaf and limb.
I am rivulets wandering the lawn.
I am flash flood ravaging dirt paths
through the pasture.
I am all streams swelling to fill Kerr Lake.
I am swelling. I am turbulence thundering
through tunnels of dams. I am rivers' confluence
roiling routes to the Atlantic. I am ocean. I am sea.
I am all oceans and seas. I am rain. I am fog.
I am teardrop remembered on the lips of the kiss at
the heart of the earth. I am mist. I am ion. I am eon.
I am song of the peeper frogs in the evening woods.
I am laughter of the skinny dippers diving from docks.
I am triumph of the cormorant soaring on wingwind
with fresh-caught fish in beak. I am breath.
I am joy. I am sorrow. I am longing.
I am then…and then again. I am flowing. I am flow.
I am not Spew Marrow Creek. I am not
Spew Marrow Creek.

In Your Place

Hoping to see you,
I looked into your sky
before gathering the comfort
of my quilt, but you
were already tucked into
the solace of clouds
among star dance, hidden
with only a hint of your glow reflecting
from snow on the ground, from the ice
on the hollies, from the know
in my heart that your fullness was on....
I heard the sing of your song and was filled
by the prowl of your howl,
by the moan of your lone, Wolf
Moon, and a smile danced the full of *my* face.

Beverly Jo Subudhi

Prosthesis

It is hard enough for me to pronounce the word, announce the word, with a lisp I
picked up from my therapist.
And I wonder what factory produced it, seduced it from its mold, the gooey gel and the exact
size and fitting and isn't it fitting that it is sent here, where I try to forget what is missing... insisting
that all is well.

The directions say to store it in its cradle, to preserve its shape and texture.
I'll label myself as an unsure observer and as a guinea pig for future inhabitants of its design.
It is hot and heavy and forgetful. It is as forgetful as I am sometimes, ... its agnostic weight
can't be described as spiritual, so I've forgotten it at massage sessions, and receive a polite
and professional call, ...your.......

In June the gel leaked from its swollen cow's eyelid, secure in its cotton pocket, on the train
from Richmond to Brooklyn, asleep in defense of its thesis.
A 36 D to a zero, in the time it takes to wait in line, on a train, to order a turkey wrap and a
Coke and chips, though Pepsi has an alliterative ring to it.
Prosthesis and trash and lisp and list and train and training bra too.
At home is the empty cradle.
At an appointment later that summer my surgeon said "you really are attached to your breast."
I asked "can I use that in a poem?"
And she said "yes."

Martha Thomas Terrell

Levitate

Ever so briefly
deep in the depths
of the tautological chorus
I am lifted off the dance in my feet
and allowed to sail with
bare arms wide as wings
my heart more full
than this tree-ringed marsh
flush with rain—

"I feel love"
just like the singer sings—
though for a moment I *am* that love
in its most profound
and human-skinned sense.

But this is not Eros—
though my husband smiles
and raises his eyebrows
at the movement emanating so
freely from my body—
This is the third kind of love
recognized by the Greeks:
Agape—and I am
for a few one-hundredths of a second
    levitating
on what I know is the laughing
and tender heart of the Divine.

Your Hand at Work

When I am west of Denver,
on any road or trail
from Montana to New Mexico,
I am awed by the amazing scope
of your western creation,
spanning horizon to horizon,
from cloud-making mountains
to narrow, stepped canyons;
from emerald-deep rivers
to unassailable hills of sand;
from star-blissed nights to
unshaded days of blue—
such magic and scale
stir me to my knees.

So I long for that drama here,
in the intimacy of lush, tall trees
and quiet, half-seen sunsets.
Let me see your majesty in the
smooth, rounded stones that
line this muddy river;
in the languid flight of herons
who winter in this wet,
marshy place of southern
sensibility and domestication—

For this is far more home than
the wondrous west can ever be—

the heart of my life in
the faces I love—

and your design of my familiar.

HIGH DEFINITION

As we reenter the woods
a tiring sun drops
behind a cloud and
the light goes flat—
which at this time of day
is magical, throwing all
into high relief:
leaves, fronds, grasses,
vines as thick as our wrists,
stones restive and impassive,
intricate cities of root.
Water and creature harmonize—
weaving this numinous
material into their songs—
All equally illuminated.
All equally shadowed.
All worthy.

Jenna Villforth Veazey

In the Starlit Night We Looked

Necks cranked back; mouths parted
puffing clouds of steamy exhaust into the frigid night
our guide calls, whoowawawa whoooohah
repeats
we listen
our cheeks still sting from the wind whipping
on the wagon ride to the middle of the forest
the silence hard to maintain
bodies shift: bellies gurgle, coats wrinkle and rustle
he calls again
we listen
the stars are like sharp sand glittered across inky indigo
only the trees stabbing upwards without their leaves look truly black
there are whispers now
hushed jokes
being stood up by nature
but after his next call
we hear a hoot back
then a flash of pale shadow flicker overhead
the barred owl answers
comes a little closer
he calls
the owl calls
flies to another branch
repeat
we are enthralled. Our guide as magic as a snake charmer
our silence is absolute
we want the magic to happen again
it never does.

D RURY W ELLFORD

L UNAR H OWLING
New York, May 22, 1991

wednesday 7 a.m.

my husband prepares for work   I roll over on my back the
     round weight of the child within   *pressing gently* my *innards* forgiving until
a sharp sudden   kick
bursts a dam
     a thin but robust deluge of liquid   I think my water just broke don't go wait
belly instantly   squeezing

taxi 9 a.m.

my husband holds me   we're 5 weeks early to the party in fear
   lack of preparation for the child arriving early *girl   boy*   a *stranger*   will it be okay
chaotic ward packed   screaming
next to me
   down the hall room by room   moans and pleas and to hell with the natural childbirth
just stop the   pain

stalled 1 p.m.

white clogs and coats scurrying   contracting not dilating start her on
     pitocin where's the fucking *anesthetic   stabbing*   my *spine*   long needle
hits a nerve   moaning
within an instant
   no longer feeling grinding pain (or legs for that matter)   I can watch *All My Children*
piece of cake   until

Phil Donahue 4 p.m.

and I cross the thin red line   too much pitocin brings back agony
   anesthesiologist is m.i.a. and *HelpMe   HelpMe*   please   *God*   what is going on
doctor hits me   up
transforming me
   into a jellyfish or a mermaid and I have no control   I can't feel a thing and nurses
tell me to   push

at 7 p.m.

"you're having a contraction now"   and I say if you say so because now I'm like an
      octopus on land legs   *slithering   uncontrollable*   not   *there*   and neither is
my nether region to   push
but I try
   in the packed ward and   my doctor like a disappointed football coach calls in an intern
to force baby   out

at 7:40 p.m.

like squeezing a tube of toothpaste and I   feeling failure hear my daughter cry a
      cry of life my life now changed forever   *weeping   tears*   of   *joy*   yet despair
and fear of   what-kind-of
mother she has
   suddenly panicked and   unprepared and desperately protective and knowing she is gentle
hoping she is   strong

before midnight

her 30-some nursery mates writhing and squirming   and the nurse says it's a-l-w-a-y-s
like this when there's a   *full   moon*   like   *lunacy*   yet it is one of nature's tidal side
effects not in our   control
I cradle her
      propped up in a hallway bed next to the nursery sea of babies   waiting for a room gazing
down at my beautiful   werewolf

ERIN NEWTON WELLS

FARM ROAD, ROUTE 10

Locals pronounce R-10 as a word, like the city in Brazil,
but flattened to sound like *Rye-o*, meddling

with its name, meddling with the earth. A forest,
then a trail. Then widened by wagons, grooves gouged.

Land cleared. An orchard once where my house stands.
Beyond it, a pasture for cows. But not now.

The road runs wider, straighter, paved, sliced
through hills. A railroad crosses beneath. Sunday morning

I hear one bell near the track, a chapel in native stone,
walls blackened by candles in sconces, kneelers

made years ago by women who lie in the churchyard
among traffic. We will lie here, plots on the map

in narrow ink, numbers by our names. We often stop
to visit ourselves. Next to us, the neighbor

who took care of our cat, the wind chime her daughter
hung from a branch. Beyond it, the cherry tree

a friend planted over her son, the earth full of us,
filled up. Beneath and around us, an orchard, pasture,

trail. Forest floor unmarked. Green sound of pines.
Go deeper. The first silence.

Of His Boat and the Lightness of Sails

He asks what I think. I see ribs curved and whispered
into place, a sleek flying thing made for air,

not seaworthy yet for the dazzle of water but smooth
as hands can shape and able for a sea of air,

able to lift and float, wanting no earthly limits. I see
sails the color of dawn, pale peach, wild air,

myself a child among sheets belled and snapped no one
thought to bring in, a branch ringing the air

on the pole as a chime or a voice calling me to follow
wherever she went, vanished into the air

as I slept. They never tell me where. They look above
at the sky. *Passed*, is what they say, like air.

Crossed over, flown, no pain or sighing, no sorrow
anymore. I want to go and find her in the air

over the trees as a bird with lightest wings, as a ship
with the lightest of sails, my arms on the air.

I want to be his boat painted sky blue, sails the color
of cloud. I hear their voices in the air

singing that day about a river over the trees, over sky
where she travels from me on a river of air.

THE GINKGO AT SHUKKEI-EN

In Hiroshima, a garden where an emperor once walked.
A tree, a shimmering yellow cloud.

For months, a simple green. Now, a sudden mellowing.
A breath. A cloud.

Everything you need to know is here. Its silent labor,
its memory of earth to make a yellow cloud.

Its root is history, ancient, enduring even the brilliant
blast, negation, a killing cloud.

Here is where they came to die, are buried, to dream
again of rivers, trees crowned in yellow cloud.

A tree, charred but alive. A garden, a river made new.
In autumn, a glory, these leaves a cloud.

Each leaf is a fan, explosion of saffron. The tree, soon
bare. But for now, this yellow cloud.

Listen. Leaf fluttering down. The world's transgression.
This tree, a magnitude trembling into cloud.

At Shukkei-en, a shaft of sun. November sky. Fish
nibbling reflection of a yellow cloud.

Frederick Wilbur

A Simple Asking

After

hunters and hounds have horned all the land,
foxing, footing, skeltering through moon woods,

after

the woodmen have chopped the farm's fuel,
the smell of acrid chips, the axe and ache, the stack,
    store, and stoke of wood,
can you
    ink my labors into the calendar of your days
as if the station of my waiting were your destination,
can you
    hear this boy's pleasing that secrets
his terrible darkness, drubbing dawn,
the sliver of his cry?

After

jackknives have whistled initials into the tree
as desire's souvenir, seriphed and shadowed,

after

my heroes have carouselled the heavens,
have meteored their verbs
into sparking, blazing, striking the anvil,

after

wings have hinged their higher blessing,
would you
    take my wounds for what they are?

After

the between of *yes* and *no*, the between of *maybe*
and *yes*, as wonderful as a gift-wrapped idea,

after

these dwindling questions, the origami fold
of map, of memory, trust of treaty hands,
will we
    know the answer of the heart?
Will we
    kiss to our haven the sheer chance, the

after

of our knowing?

Among Stones

Clearing the crumbling stone wall of creeper,
tree roots, robbing remnants to use elsewhere,
I find a Lang Brothers Whisky bottle,
spirited away by some veteran drinker half a century ago.

In shining shatters of porcelain,
nuggets of obsolete iron, the barley-brown
survivor is without chip or crack.
It has resisted the stones' nudge and settling
as they became the wild scrum they are.

In a secret cranny, as walls are
supposed to give protection separating
this from that, it long ago gave up
the man's desperate need and misplaced desire.

These scattered stones are a poor memorial
for this dead soldier as I see in ruin
a just beauty emptied of belief,
so I place it on the boulder I cannot budge
for the sun to fill it again with glow, a beacon
of comfort amid a slyly shifting world.

Denise Wilcox

Sacrament of Reconciliation

The University swallowed its shame,
made a holy confession
in front of God
and all humanity.
Students demanded a perpetual
Act of Contrition
and created
the Enslaved Laborers Memorial.
They invite the world,
you and me,
to partake of a shared penance.
Enter the circle.

Enter the circle
of gray Virginia granite.
Gray,
that nebulous color
where black and white
meet and mingle.
Gray,
the black hole in white space
where "all men are created equal"
lingers alongside the ownership of
600 lives,
enslaved to one.

Enter the circle
where pools of light
search for the North Star,
illuminate the way,
clarify the darkness,
reveal soft steady ripples of pure water.
Water of baptism
to renew faith.
Wash away the Lie.
Expose the Truth.
Acknowledge the Sin.

Can We the People,
blessed by this sacrament,
reconcile?

My Father's War

My father didn't speak
of his service
during the war.
He stuffed the horrors
deep inside and sucked the air
out like a vacuum-sealed
freezer bag.
Decades later,
the seal broke
and stories leaked out.
The memory of his fingertips
touching as he wrapped them
around a fellow soldier's
upper arm, thin to the bone
from starvation at Bataan.
The memory of his feet
ripped to shreds by coral
as he ran helter-skelter
to escape enemy strafing
on an island outpost.
The memory of his little brother
who pulled the short straw
that appointed him the one
to knife an enemy to death
in a dark tunnel on Iwo Jima.
My father plugged the leaks
with speed, uncertain
how they escaped.
The stories died,
but the memories lived.

BETH OAST WILLIAMS

KICKBALL
for Maeve Kennedy McKean and her son Gideon

First responders find both bodies underwater,
but no mention of the ball. Textured

lines, soft rubber, make it easy to catch.
Red, it's easy to see against the sky.

Third grade comes back to me, recess,
games in an open field. How we laughed

when Teresa's shoe flew off. How we cheered
when Steve rounded home.

We would have chased a foul into the river,
high-fived at the luck of a nearby boat.

We would have paddled to the drifting ball,
saved it from the bay's mounting waves,

straddled it like a flotation device
when the canoe tipped over, hugged it

like a child does a mother. Am I wrong
to wonder where the kickball blew?

A spot of red on water beacons
any head, any boat to turn. What floats

ends up still floating until it loses
all its breath, or it rides an incoming tide

and gets caught in someone's backyard.
I respond to marsh grass waving, scan

the edge of shore for a color like blood,
a broken heart, the skyburn just before night.

I Knew Better Than To Say

Friends want me to write about it,
explain how a match turns to fire
as if I'm the only one who knows
how to research insurrection.
But I'd rather write about the bird
flying south with her dinner dangling
like a little war flag from her mouth,
how she waits with a trait unknown to me,
until she's secure on a limb to eat. I'd like
to write about fears over my shoulder,
the fact that love will one day
leave me empty, like an egret
standing one-legged on a pier
looking into the river for food.
This day, nothing swims by.
Yes, I'm afraid of being left alone,
afraid I might be the pelican left behind,
my flight so pitiful I'm not even able
to follow the down of the nearest draft.
I cannot turn my head all the way around.
If I could see behind me I might
stop right here and wait. I might
run my fingers through his hair
just before sleep takes my lover away,
breathing deeply in all he exhales.
Don't ask me again to write
that this is not who we are, it is.
We are the species unable to fly,
the un-winged walkers
who every single day find a way
to pluck the idea of hope from the sky.
And once a year, we make an excuse
for all we have done by saying
Happy New Year.

KRISTIE L. WILLIAMS

PRAISE THE SCAVANGER HUNT

I've found white sand whose black underbelly
hides in the ink of my tattooed right ankle;

Live hose pipes sneaking around corners
trailing between treasure hunts and dining chair forts
reinforced with Oreos and homemade magic;

Wood carved backscratchers and crank-turn
ice cream churns:

Grapevines and clotheslines witnessing
fried bologna sandwiches picnicking with Duke's mayonnaise
under the apple tree;

Dry roasted salted peanuts
begging to be sipped from a glass bottle
"baby" coke

Backdoor flip-flops fighting to free themselves
from corn silks still doggin' their heels;

Fatback, collard greens and cast-iron-skillet cornbread lures
baiting Santa's bounty far better than any kitchen
concocted cookie ever could;

Shoeboxes bustin' at the seams with
Used-to-Coulds… Do Whaaats?!!? And *Oh My Souls*;

Countertops inundated with deep fried door-stoppin'
Crazy-Christian casseroles;

Seasoned with *Jesus is Watching You*
and *Don't Forget Bedtime Prayers;*

Washed down with
Don't Think You Can Talk To Him
desserts;

Half-full jars of *Grandma's Molasses* waging war against Motown melodies
oozing along the outer edges of a Percy Sledge groove… An arsenal aimed
at keepin' dem knees stuck together;

Fires I started with a dead level stare
and the still smoldering ashes spit from my tongue

Shattered mirrors that cut me loose
from the singular view feminine elders
used to frame me

Praise the needle and thread that patched
these pieces of being

Blessed be the quilt that
steels my soul

Diana Woodcock

No Death
> "The smallest sprout shows there is really no death."
> *Song of Myself*, Section 6, Walt Whitman

Stuck in a traffic jam
on a Doha street, I seek
relief and find it

in a weed sprouting from a crack
in the median strip pavement.
One continuous, indigenous weed

just what I need to reassure me
all shall be well, just as Julian
of Norwich wrote. Instead

of ranting with all my fellow
commuters, I give thanks
for a persistent weed,

enjoy the simple beauty
and pluck of a plant
refusing to die.

And so must I,
though this aggressive,
progressive, over-developing city

threatens to pave right over me.
Its slave I will not be.
This little visible weed

revealing the invisible protector
of the weak, the divine power
moving for all time through all

creation. What liberation
these thoughts provide
as I finally drive

on to my destination,
feeling empowered somehow
by a simple sprout. And isn't this

what living's all about—thriving
in the most difficult, unlikely,
inhospitable conditions?

Refusing, till the time comes—
not at one's own bidding—
to lay down one's tired bones?

Which, with any luck, will be dug up
to nourish some creature
or cause native plants to flourish.

To Life
    "May what I do flow from me like a river,
    no forcing and no holding back,
    the way it is with children." Rainer M. Rilke

To realize—to tap into—
that direct line to the divine.

To reverence creation—
make of each new sunrise
a celebration.

To let being not doing
be my priority,
make silence my preference.

To be filled with *ruthless
compassion,** ears perceptive
to suffering cries,
yet practice the peace
of detachment.

To leave the weeds—
dandelions, mustard,
goldenrod—for the bees.

To bless, as St. Francis did
the sow, each creature
I'm honored to know.

To see with my heart
the invisible, believe
the unbelievable.

So much can go wrong--
To sing a song of thanksgiving
for all this is right.

To take time to arrange
flowers in a vase,
fruit on the windowsill.

To keep still or pace
with the snail in spite
of the world's ceaseless spinning.

To make losing my goal—
money, possessions, obsessions—
finally realizing cashing in's
not all it's cracked up to be.

To be able, finally,
to say with acknowledgement
and full acceptance,

C'est la vie!

*Trungpa Rinpoche

KATHERINE E. YOUNG

DRIVING TO JUNIATA
for David Hutto

Up there's the interstate, peeping through trees.
Down here among hollows, satellite dishes,
a man on his deck guzzles beer, wishes
he were driving that highway. His fancy speeds
past the graveyard of riding mowers, the three-
foot ceramic gnome squatting on the lawn
beside a cabin whose mailbox reads "Yablonski"—
speed's his algorithm for life, for freedom.
I don't know where America lives, but I know
in my bones she's down here, among red-lacquered
barns, weed-choked byways, plank bridges.
She bleeds through the landfills, the tiered ridges
of doublewides, the hand-lettered placards
with directions to Jesus. Be patient. Go slow.

THE BEAR

i.

The bear marauds inside my garden,
plants his tracks among the roses;
his scent lingers in the hollies, the yews.
I gather broken branches in my arms,
pocking hands and face with prickling leaves.
Inside the house, my cats sniff anxiously,
note the bitter tang of bear on my skin.
They press their noses to the window,
seeking solace in the glass:
clear-eyed frame that holds us back,
bladed pane that keeps us safe.

ii.

The bear says: "I'm not dangerous!
Let me make a den for you:
I'll decorate the walls with shells,
spread soft moss across your bed;
songs of falling water will soothe the air.
Sometimes—perhaps—I'll kiss
your full, pleading lips,
though they're not the type
to which I'm accustomed."

iii.

I tell the bear: "My prince
will come claim me." Clear, uninflected.
The bear just laughs:
"Does his skin smell of musk,
his flesh taste of honey?
Does his fur warm you in winter?
Does he know to smooth your cheek
with all his claws drawn in?"

iv.

When he holds me in his arms,
I hear roaring in my ear.

v.

The bear says, "Look closely:
there's a ring set in my nose."
And though I've stroked his snout
a thousand times, I've never—before now—
felt iron beneath my fingers.
Says the bear, "Once, I begged
for my living, recited rhymes,
my paw outstretched.
I screwed the ring in myself,
thought I'd live better with a chain,
with four walls to steady me."

vi.

The bear shambles through crowds,
snout turning side to side,
his eyes always seeking,
I don't know what he's seeking….
He prefers I fall two steps back,
that way no one shouts, "Look!
A woman's chained to that bear!"
Although the chain's invisible.
Although at night, when he leads me out,
no one sees he's a bear.

Laura Younger

172 Davis Street

I

Inside, Grandpa raps on the porch window,
Finger raised in warning, a minor deity,
Daedalus to the cousins' Icarus,
warning against the climb towards the sun.
We freeze, wayward demigods, oblivious
to the dangers of the rotting coop—
our boost to the lower limbs of the vast
Chestnut tree.

The world was bigger then.

Halted in our hubris, we
run shrieking from censure,
until a new game evolves;
Siege of Troy, slingshots for trebuchets,
horse chestnuts, still in their spiked pods
like naval mines, vault wildly
through the soft fall air
until one meets its mark,
and the victim dissolves in tears.

II

Our pipefitter uncle of the practical joke
has us trapped on the sofa,
showing his photos of the 'poo factory.'
His pride in his work pins us in place.
We don't dare show boredom; besides,
the scatological humor keeps our attention.
Beautifully rendered photos
of pipes, steel, a harsh industrial landscape
repel and fascinate at the same time.

"Quick, pull my finger!"

III

Aunt Joanne and Uncle John always
show up late.
The meal is cooked, the table set,
everyone well into their pre-dinner cups.
They dazzle, shine in their perfect suburban polish,
but must dash early; there's the baby to get to bed,
a charity meeting and work in the morning,
so sorry we can't help with the dishes.

Harbinger

In a sweetly pungent,
mulch-strewn,
grass-mown,
red summer sunset,
you pause.

Feel that first
cool late-August breeze—
Autumn's breath.
Clouds sharpen themselves
on cerulean sky.
Trees of dusty green
take their last gasp of summer,
turning, turning.

SALLY ZAKARIYA

STAR LIGHT, STAR BRIGHT
"The universe is under no obligation to make
sense to you." Neil deGrasse Tyson

I never asked the stars to spell your name
or said the sun should rise especially for us,
and when the full moon went into eclipse
I never thought night darkened just for us
and us alone.

There's something to be said for planets,
how they ride their measured rings
around the sun, and something to be said
for meteorites, those rocky tears
the cosmos sheds.

But let science say what can be said
about it all—it makes no sense to me.
I watch in wonder as the heavens
wheel and drink it in, enthralled.

So when you talk of perihelion
or perigee, event horizon or
ecliptic, I nod, then smile inside
and think, how lucky that the stars
aligned for us.

MISSING THE LUNAR ECLIPSE

Asleep at four AM, we missed
the moon's eclipse this time.
And the universe went on
without us—went on its precise
mathematical way, pacing
its predetermined steps,
maintaining its proper
distances, simply being—
as though we don't exist
at all.

And why not? We are
no more than tiny specks
on a small planet—insignificant
yet somehow convinced we
matter. To ourselves at least,
and to our fragile world.

Awake, we watch the skies
from time to time, note
clouds and stars, even trace
the phases of the moon.

And who's to say the moon's
not watching us, tracing
our recurring phases of war
and peace, unsettled by our
violence and greed, fearful
we'll export our strife
out past the atmosphere
that cloaks us.

Try not to worry, moon.
We'll do our best, our puny
human best, so long as you
still sail imperfect circles
in the sky.

THE POETRY SOCIETY OF VIRGINIA

THE

CENTENNIAL ANNIVERSARY

ANTHOLOGY

1923 - 2023

PART TWO

POEMS FROM PRIOR ANTHOLOGIES

LYRIC VIRGINIA TO-DAY

MARY SINTON LEITCH, EDITOR

1932

SELECTED POEMS

Lawrence Lee

The University of Virginia

He who conceived you lived upon a hill
And read the skies, the earth, good books, and men.
Of all this wisdom gathered to his will
He built that he might walk the world again.
They who have loved the earth have served it best;
He breathed its air, rode through Virginia mud,
Beheld the mornings, and her starry west,
A stallion's zest for being in his blood.

Now autumn blows red leaves across his grave,
The crocus finds his mountain perch in spring;
Yet, though he feels no changing season near,
He stirs among these captured dreams that save;
Endless shall be for him awakening
In the unsaddled young who pasture here.

For any Lady's Birthday

Spring's silver poplars stand apart
Most ladylike of trees,
And mortal ladies should take heart
From gentlefolk like these.

They watch the blue days pass along,
They see the nights go by,
But keep forever morning's song
And night-time's starry sky.

They know the maiden spring goes soon,
But their wise hearts are still;
For they have seen the quiet moon
Above a wooded hill.

The poplars wear a halo guise
Their silver crown of years,
And if all ladies were as wise
There would be fewer tears.

Mary Sinton Leitch

One Rose

I cannot bear the beauty of one rose,
Therefore I pray you give me two or three-
A nosegay of them, that my eyes may be
Distracted and not linger over-long
On one: its heart holds too much mystery:
Within it burns the holy vestal fires
Of all the world's deep longing and desires:
All loveliness is there! So soft among
Those tender petals such perfection glows,
I cannot bear the beauty of one rose.

The Swallow

While you lay dying, at your door
The chill rain beat: above the field
That sloped to meet the wind-swept shore
A lonely swallow wheeled.

Dumbly I watched the swallow, I
Heard unaware your failing breath:
Those strong wild wings against the sky
Pulsed through my thoughts of death.

Strange, strange that memory now denies
Your face to all my yearning pain,
And yields instead of dying eyes
A swallow in the rain.

Virginia Taylor McCormick

A Star for Tea

Always there must be two of me;
One seeking after beauty.
One who walks with lowered eyes
Upon the path of duty.

Always there must be two of me;
One with dancing feet,
Who gathers crimson poppies
While the other garners wheat.

Always there must be two of me:
Half saint, half sinner;
One must go forth to meet my Lord,
One stay to mind the dinner.

But I hope when death comes to me
That Martha will be gone,
So I may trip as Mary
Over Heaven's daisied lawn.

Forgetting dishes Martha washed,
Her calm expediency,
I'll drink the sky's blue loveliness
And pick a star for tea.

Virginia Moore

My Father

Because of him I cannot say this world
Is weary, or a failure, or a fraud,
Or that a lovely vessel must be flawed,
Or that the hopeful mind is not as brave
As any daring action that we laud.

Because of him I cannot say the fall
Is sad, or that the winter is too hard,
Or that the spring by transiency is marred,
Or that the summer in its natural fields
Already by the coming frost is scarred.

Because of him whose mind is more my sire
Than body, and whose heart has been my grace,
I cannot say man, whom years efface,
Is not the strong effacer in the end
Of all that's selfish, trivial and base.

Joan of Arc

I have no solid horse to share with Joan,
I have no wit to contradict a duke
If there were dukes; I dream my dream alone,
And cannot in the face of Rome's rebuke
Consider them divine. Rather I know
That nations are not worth the men they break,
And tardy Joans are destined to forego
Danger, and the incentive of the stake.

But I shall ride—most surely I shall ride—
Across a field more difficult than France,
Sternly, upon a horse that is my pride
And make my sword of each foul circumstance
To conquer half the world disdainfully
Before a world prescribed can conquer me.

John Richard Moreland

Lament

O yesterday her hands were white
As butterflies among the bright
Red zinnias in her garden-plot!
Today her hands are just as white.
But all their motion is forgot.

O yesterday the velvet hue
Of her dear eyes was clear and blue
As seas where slender palm trees grow:
Today her eyes are just as blue,
But like dark violets under snow.

O yesterday her voice to me
Was gold and silver melody
Like birds that waken with the dawn:
Today I wait expectantly ....
The music of her voice is gone.

Wind and Sea

The wind is a teasing hunger,
The sea is a quenchless thirst,
And I am a moon-marked dreamer
By wind and wave accurst—

With never a place to linger,
Or hide from the seeking sea,
But the curve of a thin, blue finger
Continually beckons me.

With never a hill or hollow
To harbor me safe and sure,
But the wind, hound-like, will follow
And sniff at my bolted door:

Or set the casement shaking
Till quiet or rest is vain,
Till the sound of water…breaking…
Make me its slave again.

Florence Dickinson Stearns

Old Walls

I understand the language of old walls,
And in the chambers of my heart, they spread
Their rich equivalent. My heart's own halls
Are musical with words that they have said.

I mind a grey wall in an ancient town.
From off its ledge, soft spoken in a breeze,
The ivy let its cautious streamers down
To drowse and wake beside catalpa trees.

The light so loved this wall, in chequered play
It tripped with shade upon its weathered plane,
And you had heard, if you had chanced that way,
The sparrows rustling in its cloistered lane.

I've lagged its length along, when moon-possessed,
It wore a silver veil and seemed to be
A place where beauty was a finished quest
That made an end of all uncertainty.

Old wall, so mellow and so satisfying,
No matter what of turmoil life may bring,
You shed a peace, you make a brave replying
To doubt, to fear, to every storm-tossed thing.

Lyric Virginia To-Day

Volume II

Mary Sinton Leitch, Editor

1956

Selected Poems

CARLETON DREWRY

THE ANCIENT ANGER

Though lightning lash from the sky,
And lunge, and plow this planet
And plunge all lives upon it,
Not from this threat nor its thunder
Emptying echoes under
Do we finally die.

Not from elemental riot
Nor sudden celestial stroke,
But through some nerve that broke
Between all body and mind,
Causing the world to go blind,
Do we grow cold and quiet

Who once with a torn tongue
Cried in the wilderness, heard
Ourselves saying the tortured Word,
The immortal hope of heaven
From our mortal hearts wrung,
Whose answer, ungiven,

Broke our faith in the sky,
With the fear of its violence:
Not from the old swift anger,
But of our slow mortal hunger,
And the sinister sneer of silence,
The long insult of silence,
Do we utterly die.

Leigh Hanes

Morning Song

Oh, the light's an eon winging
  from the star an eon gone,
But the stuff that keeps man singing
  is the breaking of the dawn,

And the hoping and the dreaming
  through the grit and grime and grief,
And the sunken island gleaming
  in an atoll of belief!

Old Fence Post

The old fence post that tilts awry
Was never a thing to hold the eye,
Till one fine day in a nervous flit
A wren flew out of the heart of it!

A tiny hole was all I could see
But much, so much was hidden from me

That now, whenever I pass that way,
I tip my hat to a very fine day,
And an old fence post, and a little brown wren
That may any moment fly out again!

BRODIE HERNDON

HERRING FOR MY GRANDFATHER

Roe herring was Grandfather's wish;
Roe herring was his chosen dish.
"Fit for the best of men," he said,
"Is herring and hot batter bread."

The Chesapeake, James, and Rappahannock;
Chickahominy, York, and the Potomac
Gave roe herring to soothe his hunger
Until it seemed they could no longer.

There was no doubt this *aqua manna*
Might bless the Hudson or Susquehanna.
From Kennebeck and Penobscot some might be deducted;
But Grandfather had never been reconstructed.

"Up North, the fish," Grandfather swore,
"Are nervous and skinny;" and he was sure
This urge of production in Northern waters
Was not directed toward herring daughters.

All herring unequipped with roe,
Grandfather thought malapropos;
And it was not without compunction
He acknowledged the male to have a function.

Grandfather bows his grizzled head
Over the fish and batter bread.
He says a grace for both the dishes,
But special praise for herring fishes.

Josephine Johnson

Evening Prayer

The air was palpable with gold
Too brimming for the sky to hold
As burnished oak leaves, one by one,
Held up a mirror to the sun.
The birds above the mountain rim
Were cherubim and seraphim,
Lifting translucent wings in flight
Against the radiance of light.
No smallest whisper seemed to stir
The invisible threads of gossamer
Laid on the lawn, yet rainbows ran
Shimmering from span to span.
Midges and gnats with rise and fall
Moved to an ancient ritual
In gauzy dance. O King of Kings,
It was the hour of humble things!
The small sweet clover, magnified,
Beheld the Bridegroom, *was* the Bride,
And every lowly plantain head
Was haloed by the glory spread.

Then, lifting high each shining sword,
The grass stood up and praised the Lord!

Ruby Altizer Roberts

Remembering a Brother

I never see a fair-haired farmer boy
Furrow a field but it is always you.
Keen memory fills my heart with pain and joy
When brown fields ripple under skies of blue.

I used to tread behind you step by step
With bare feet sinking into satin ground.
Daylong, though sun beat down, the pace I kept
Knowing that dusk would see us homeward bound.

I watched blue acres of the sky last night
And saw cloud furrows line in wave on wave.
I marked a falling star in blazing flight
And shivered at the ecstasy it gave:

Thinking of you, I wondered if up there
You ploughed the heavens; kept the meadows fair.

Nancy Byrd Turner

The Ballad of Captain Kemble

Captain Kemble of Boston town
Sat in the stocks with frost on his coat
And ice in his hair and a song in his throat,
And none of his scorners could scorn him down.
Shame on a seaman scarce ashore
Who publicly, lewdly, Lord's Day noon
Kissed his wife at his own front door!
He sat in the stocks and made a tune.

"O the skies were drear as ton elder's brow,
Ho, my hearties!" He bawled with a grace;
"And a stout sea serpent rolled over my prow,
But I steered by the star of a woman's face.
The wind was wild as a tiger's lust,
It shattered the dark with fierce alarms—
'Twould have blown you clods to a whiff of dust,
But it blew me straight to the port of her arms."

They tightened the cleats in the frozen wood
And tilted his head for sharper pains.
"So I sailed," he cried, "With a flame in my blood
Would have curdled the milk in your flabby veins.
There was death in the waves and hell in the blast,
And the Devil spanking from north to south,
But Lord's Day harbored me home at last
And blessed my brine with the sweet of her mouth!"

So bold and blatant his ballad rang
That the judges huddled their women back.
"If beauty be sin, good wives," he sang,
"Ye'll send no man to the pinch o' the rack!"
And they set him free while they counselled whether
God or the law should fix his doom….
But the morning stars all chortled together
High in the dawn, and squired him home.

THE GOLDEN ANNIVERSARY

ANTHOLOGY

BESS B. GRESHAM, EDITOR

1973

SELECTED POEMS

BESS B. GRESHAM

REQUIEM

I heard harsh sounds from where I stood,
Like breaking up old mellow wood.
My father standing quiet by
Gave answer to my frenzied cry:
This truth came like a sacrilege
Impelling me to save the bridge.
But now the bridge was torn apart;
I felt the nails rip through my heart.
And all at once I could not stand:
I sank upon the river's sand.
Then father spoke—so soft and low
"All things old—must sometime—go."

MORNING PRAYER

Give breadth to my sight that I may see
more clearly the things surrounding me.
Make keen my ears that I may hear
the sounds of bird-wings flitting near.
Grant depth to my heart that I understand
better the heart of every man.
Give strength to my hands and to my mind
that I may bless the tasks I find.

Grace Pow Simpson

I Must Have a Place

I could not see him reduced to ash. Let
It happen underground, if it must,
An ecclesiastical return to dust.
I must have a place upon this earth square
Enough to stand upon
And say he is from here to here. Yet
I hate this narrow
Architecture
Down to the marrow
Gray stones,
Down to the milk
White bones,
Down to the silk
Lined box that my mother poor.
He should lie
At home in the side yard where
He used to sit in beneficent sun.
There is little comfort in the stare
Of crumbling angels row on row
And granite cannot hold his history;
Still I choose this over nothing. I
Must have a place of absolute geography
Where my father is, where of necessity
I go.

Bruce Souders

A Beethoven Commemoration ... 1970

A mighty rocket
hurled by tempestuous furies
beyond the pull of gravity,
you pioneered new worlds of beauty
fraught in shapes of sound
unheard by defenders of conventions
unsuited to your untamed genius.

Nursed by solitude and suffering,
your Faustian soul,
defying petty prophecies of men,
cried *Eroicas* of bitter disappointment
and crescendoed to full-throated *Freudes*
that embraced the millions of a world
whose applause you could not hear.

Hounded by the frailties of body and soul
that make their bed with sons of Time and Space,
and cut asunder from those who loved you most
by that sharp swordsman in your mouth,
you have found your peace in the company of the Muses,
where nothing is required of you
but to amplify your songs throughout Eternity.

Ulrich Troubetzkoy

Upland Grave: Lincolnville, Maine

Elnora, Alice and Emery
were children who once loved the sea,
who hoarded shining stones and shells
and listened for the channel bells.
They had explored the secret caves
made hollow by the swirling waves,
caught starfish and sea urchins, spied
anemones below the tide.
Barefooted on the flats they found
the live sand dollars, brittle, round,
went clamming in the blue-gray mud
and swimming in the cove at flood.

Elnora, Alice and Emery,
only the pines repeat the sea
across this landfall of the dead,
though here are sumacs turning red
and the lonely acreage of God
bears pink spirea, goldenrod.
Perhaps you climbed this hill before,
along its pathway from the shore.
Perhaps you crumbled this sweet fern
not thinking how you would return,
and gaily leaping this stone wall
heaped blueberries in cap and shawl,
not dreaming that the place would keep
this granite silence of your sleep.

Virginia Lyne Tunstall

Nostalgia

I know this town is a fine town,
  But once I used to be
Where I could watch the ships go out,
  And the ships come home from sea.

There's never a sight in city streets
  Though they be wide and gay,
There's never a sight in city streets
  Like a great ship under way.

With the staunch pride in the heart of her
  As she follows the running trails,
Her rudder lost in the wreathy foam,
  And the west wind in her sails.

And there's never a sight that I can see
  In all this crowded place,
Like a dancing schooner, homeward bound,
  With the sunset in her face!

So what care I for your city streets,
  And what are her sights to me?
I used to watch the ships go out,
  And the ships come home from sea!

Legacy

I thought, awake and restless on my bed,
  Within a world asleep,
If dying, I could take one thing from life,
  What would I care to keep?

Courage and faith and hope—these all are good.
  Strong is the staff of pride.
But I would choose the tears of one who loved me,
  Falling the night I died.

Catharine Morris Wright

American Spring

And will the Catbird sing again,
The Catbird, garrulous and long;
With no unusual note of pain,
No anguish in his song?

The birds of Holland shiver still;
Scattered and spare are those of France;
The English raven parts his bill
But makes no utterance.

While over every field and wood
Which rains of April saturate,
The season ties an early snood
Of violets from gate to gate.

Where nothing hampers nature here,
And it abundantly complies,
The Catbird tosses up his clear
Spontaneous, melodic cries.

Exults and ravages the air,
This moment in especial whim—
Quickly put fear, no matter where,
Aside, for just an interim!

Commit it to a cherry root;
Beneath a hawthorne or a shad
Conceal its constant and acute
Insinuation, and be glad!

Beneficent for those who die,
For those alive and those to be,
Is one heart's opening once, to cry
In concert with such melody.

Anthology of Poems

by

Member Poets

Bess B. Gresham, Editor

1985

Selected Poems

Lois Sanger McGuffin

Butterflies Are Free—Or Are They?

Like the butterfly, I waited long in the chrysalis.
Changing from ugly worm into a thing of beauty,
I burst forth to stretch my wings,
My beautiful butterfly wings.
To soar on soft breezes with great joy,
To reach for the sun
And to sip nectar from fragrant flowers.
This is ecstasy, this is fulfillment.
But the chrysalis calls me back,
It claims I owe my allegiance there.
It needs me back inside.
How can I get back into the chrysalis?
These wings will not fold again;
They will break—smash into a thousand pieces.
I will be a broken thing back in the chrysalis;
I will die.
The pull of the chrysalis is strong,
And so is the pull of the sun.
I am torn in two.
I want to use my wings;
I don't want them broken.
The chrysalis still calls me to return.
How can I go back? How can I refuse?
Please, chrysalis, understand.
Please let me be free.
I want to live!

James McNally

The Lefthanded Raker

My grandmother was trapped once
By a field fire but escaped.
She ran toward an opening
That soon closed.
Flames closed behind her.
Her father would not allow
Her to rake lefthanded.
I rake lefthanded, too, strumming
The tines scratchily over
Many leathery oakleaf clusters
Sliding to their last mission
Across the thin green lawn.
I can go on raking lefthanded.
We live in a many-sided land.
War fares elsewhere for a while,
We live where, how we please,
Though still wonder at
The use of leaves,
Which way the fire will turn,
How to handle the self.
Or many fingers of the rake.
Many have raked
And gone.
We remain to rake
In the grand old relay
Of give and take.

Evelyn Ritchie

The Lights Came on, November 12, 1938

Children, that was the day
We squinted at the kitchen clock
In the close evening with the stove
Too nervous-hot and Mama stirring
The fried potatoes to pieces
As she stood first on one
Broken shoe then the other.
I was laying down five Sunday plates
Watching Daddy in the doorway
Worry about his Sears sockets
And thirty dollars' worth of wiring
He'd crawled about the attic to install.
Brothers Lowell and Larry
Turned switches on and off and on,
Turned on each other,
Turned somersaults, turned serious
When the hands stroked seven—
Maybe the old clock's wrong
The wiring short
The day mistaken
Maybe we can't pay
Two-fifty every month.
But out on the porch a meter
Buzzed soft as growing corn
And a flash floated us in light
As we laughed and jumped together
To blow the lamp out.

Shirley Nesbit Sellers

On Standing before a House on Freemason Street

Stand just so that you face the kitchen garden,
Enclosed with rustic fence and blossomed hedge,
Where lichened trunks and tireless clinging creeper
Support the sundial's bid to vanquish time.

Stand just so that beneath your feet you feel
The smoothed, uneven cobbles of the street
And at the very moment catch a glimpse
Of massive door presiding in its brass
Above the steep stone steps that bound its base.

Step upward, if you must, but turn away
From modern travesties of sound and sight
And hear the silence of the ivy tell
How sun-laid bricks have slept beneath the vine
And hidden their red past in soft green leaves;
And hesitate before you venture on!

Enchantment of a century ago
May lose allurement when you turn the knob.
The charm is standing here alone and still,
Between the unreal sureties of today
And yesterday's inimitable dream.

Florence Davidson Strother

The Tall Ships

The tall ships entered the harbor.
On the edge of the pier an old woman stood
Relishing the salt spray upon her wrinkled face
While close by a small boy looked hard
Upon the tree-like masts.
The scene conjured many thoughts, thoughts of jewels held
In unattainable caches
And heavy winds that threw the ships
And broke their masts.
Of strange fins and globes of whales
Breaking the surface.
Waning moons and surging tides
And metallic suns slipping like
Coins into a slotted sea.
Tales of treachery and greed and ominous
Long walks upon a slimy plank into the
Murky depth.
The child wore upon his head a wide elastic band
Supporting two tall crimson feelers.
On the ends of the wand-like antennae small
Sparkling balls rotated as he chewed his bubble gum.
When the wind filled the sails and the flags grew taut
The boy moved closer and his eyes filled with awe and joy.
They stood—suspended—timeless—
An old woman and a would-be pirate boy.

Henry Taylor

Projectile Point, Circa 2500 B.C.

In the garden in high summer as the sun dropped,
I worked my hoe in short scythe-swings
until one stroke turned a pebble I stopped to pick up.
I stood pinching it, thumbing off earth crumbs;

this has happened before, but not to me.
There were dozens of these in a black japanned box
in my grandfather's bedroom, which was also
his grandfather's bedroom. In the days when men

plowed the fields behind horses sunup to sundown
watching the furrow open up and lie over,
three paces ahead of their feet, there was time
to reach down midstride and pocket a recognized stone.

At such times a man might fall to imagining,
but why not stick to such facts as may be?
It is broken at tip and base: botched,
chipped at the end of a shaft-flight,

or lost until it broke under the plow;
and such facts as there are now include
one hot afternoon when I stood sole-deep
in soft ground, wondering at the four thousand years

between the two men who had touched this stone,
guessing how it was not to care
for the magic I felt flowing out of it,
but just to stand here, touching only an implement

like a hoe or a pitchfork, watching the ground
as I watched it, not thinking of the sun
moving on as it moved over me, as it will
when the rocks and the water are alone here again.

1993

ANTHOLOGY

OF

THE POETRY SOCIETY OF VIRGINIA

OLGA KRONMEYER, EDITOR

SELECTED POEMS

Joseph Awad

Watching Snowflakes Fall

Milling in the street lamp's aureole,
They glitterdance, they swirl—adagios
Of dazzle—down the night.
Borne by requiems of wind
To dark suburban cemeteries,
One by one.
Where hoary angels keep the wake,
They take their rest—
Each silent flake.

Winds tonight will shoulder more
Than Palomar has stars,
Or the unnumbered leaves blown
In blustery November dusk.
Random crystals,
Microphotographed, reveal
Art gratuitous, in miniature, exact
Originals,
The signature intact.

They sweep a barren tundra, steep the night
Of prairies, woods and mountain ranges
For a thousand miles, and have for ages,
Where there is none to wonder at their numbers,
Their separate,
Their fretwork perfectness,
For whom to catalogue or sing?
Whose regret
Or remembering?

George Garrett

A Suit for Mr. Charlie
—from LIVES OF THE POETS: A SATIRE

All the bright and shiny
scissors of a certain village
in Croatia are marching, marching.

The scissors are marching proudly,
followed by thimbles, needles and thread,
directly to Durham, New Hampshire.

Meanwhile in the windy and treeless
highlands of faraway Scotland
a significant number of sheep

have given up their fleece to make
the tweed which soon enough these tools
will make into something wonderful.

It will become a suit,
an elegant and sturdy tweed suit,
especially made for Charley Simic.

The fabric like its source
is docile and cooperative,
but (alas) not all the tailors

of Yugoslavia have taught
obedience to the scissors and needles.
These things will quarrel, and the suit

will turn out very strange.
To wear it at all Simic
will have to drag his right leg along

as if it were wooden and longer
than the other one, will have to shrug
his right shoulder and twist his left arm

behind his back. "Look at that poor man,"
a New Hampshire lady will whisper.
"But what a beautiful suit!"

Keppel Hagerman

Wish You Were Here

Your postcards start arriving now,
vibrate with mammoth palms, magenta sunsets.
Honolulu is heaven you write,
wish you were here.
I'm staying home this winter
so you'll have a place to send the pretty cards;
I'll answer them
to tell you what you're missing.

It snowed last week,
the chickadees and flakes
all flew together.
I stayed inside, marveled at
my complete happiness.
While you fish for mahi-mahi,
stand beside a waterfall,
I play Copeland, read Thoreau,
smell beef and red wine
simmering in the kitchen.

Today in the mail, along with your card,
a seed catalogue arrives.
In sub-zero weather
I can sniff roses
and the lavender perfume of lilac.
You say you'll stay until the winter's over;
the first crocus will be long gone
when you come home.

OLGA KRONMEYER

A POSTSCRIPT TO SYLVIA'S SAVAGE GOD
"I do not want a plain box, I want a sarcophagus,
   With tigery stripes, and a face on it . . ."

I want a casket with a skylight
High and long enough
That I can pull
Myself up and kneel,
Then poke my head out
And greet footsteps
With free verse.

I want the midnight chill
To ring through the skylight
Like crystal prisms swinging
On a gold chandelier;
To brush my neck and hair;
To blue my egg-shell nails
That I can blow them flesh-pink
With a blind poet's finger-tipped dawn.

I do not want my casket
Borne within a stone house
Bearing an unburdened cross
On which three sparrows speak
Blank verse. Set me down light
On stamped dirt, not within walls
Papered with tiger skins,
But tinted with sun-greened glass.

Place me near wooden flats
Of low milkweed, where northern suns
Set and rise in the south.
Pipes drain liquid similes,
Monarch metaphors mount a black madonna
While gold birds roost outside the greenhouse.

Margaret Ward Morland

Bits and Pieces

Fall came in bits and pieces this year—a blue
porcelain sky cracked by a slingshot sun,
a shot of fire exploding in a velvet
of green, a shock of gold where none had been
before, the wind's knife-edge bared once or twice,
leaves the color of bruises shrouding the ground,
the crickets telling it all, if I'd listened.

It's one thing to lose your mother, but to lose
her in bits and pieces—terror crazing her face
like porcelain when she strays into that other
room where barbwire chaos cages order
just out of reach—is another. Fingering
her scarf, my gracious lady asks about
the children. I start telling how when the leaves
let go, her toddler great-grand plays catch with
the wind. But she is listening somewhere else,

and I am remembering the Ming bowl wrapped
in silk and carried out of China by
my husband slipping from the Japanese
and Mao, how, long after, our daughter's two-year
hands unguarded carried it and slipped,
its luminescence shattered into bits
and pieces—over and done, irreparable.

What cleaner mourning to sweep up the bits
and pieces telling memories, or rake
the leaves for next spring's compost, than to fold
the raveling shawl with all its ragged edges,
the bright-colored shawl that time gone kept me warm.

Dabney Stuart

The Writing Machine

I sleep in it.
It's a cross between an iron lung
and an incubator, varying in size
according to my fear of being seen.
It affords me no physical
nourishment or warmth.
It's like a Sabbath
in that it enables worship
but isn't an object of it.
Its light
helps me to read fine print
at two hundred feet, depth or distance,
and to figure out which of the world's
rejection slips are love letters.
I accumulate a rhythm
in its body similar to the heart's
beat in mine, complete with tics
and pauses: I hear it telling
how loss dies into sweetness, dies
into the next mouth that will speak
its living. I hear it lodge
the stone into the lion's throat.
Yet in spite of every appearance
I know it does nothing but enclose me,
a cocoon, a spun self,
a way of becoming.
Without it I would never wake up.

THE POETRY SOCIETY OF VIRGINIA

80TH ANNIVERSARY

ANTHOLOGY OF POEMS

JOSEPH AWAD, EDITOR

2003

SELECTED POEMS

Patsy Anne Bickerstaff

Collection

I was a dreadful mother to these dolls:
Dressed in each other's gowns, they watched my plays;
They romped outside in mud, and lost their shoes.
I taught them splits and back bends, braided wigs,
Pushed them in carriages, took them to bed.
For Christmas, I would have them new again:
Restrung, their paint retouched, ringlets replaced;
Wearing fresh frocks, from Mama's magic hands.
I clean them now, and smooth their thinning curls,
Wash clothing, make new dresses one more time.
Retired at last, they sit along the shelf,
Their aprons filled with childhood, eyes as bright
As Mama's on so many Christmas Eves;
Their fingers scarred by pups' and babies' teeth.
A few cross-eyed or lame; but they all smile,
And I remember every accident,
Each playmate, game, and summer afternoon.

Rosellen's Alexander dolls were kept
In glass, to decorate her perfect room.
She never played in dirt, or ran in woods,
Or soiled her pinafore, or mussed her hair.
She dusted now and then, to keep her dolls
As pristine as herself. When she grew up,
She sold them. They were worth much more than mine.

Phyllis Hall Haislip

Spading the Garden

That hot, still day,
my father and I worked together.
He turned the earth
with a spade
and I, trudging after him,
shook the soil from the sod.

Sweat streamed from my father's forehead
and dripped off the end of his nose.
Damp stains,
like continents in a geography book,
grew on his soiled undershirt.

The just-turned earth,
felt cool on my bare feet,
and I didn't mind
the clouds of earth that flew
from the beaten clods
and settled on my shirt and shorts.

Clang, clatter, scrape.
My father paused and bending down,
brushed off an oblong, dun-colored stone.
He stuck the spade in the ground,
took out his handkerchief,
and mopped his brow.

As we rested there in the sun,
I suddenly knew,
although I was only seven,
that if I lived one hundred years
this exact moment
would never come again.
So I fixed it forever
like a stone
in the soil of memory.

ROBERT L. KELLY

PAVAROTTI IN THE BATH

Bathrooms force the truth on me.
Mirrors reflect just what they see,
Showing with reality
Life's ephemerality.

Bathrooms are too grim for me
Without Luciano's soaring C.
I pick a tape, it's heaven sent,
"Daughter of the Regiment."

Nine high Cs all in a row,
Just can't wait to start the show
Eight high Cs he sings out bold,
Ninth high C he wants to hold.

Birds outside all cease to sing
Just to hear that high C ring,
Swelling, swelling, louder, longer,
His perfect C gets stronger, stronger,

Shaking mirror, plaster, lath,
Soaring sound fills the bath,
Until my wife pounds on the door
And I, breathless, fall to floor.

Struggling to my feet I say,
"Perfect way to start the day,
Improved at least by nine and a half,
With Pavarotti in the bath."

Carolyn Kreiter-Foronda

Lately I Have Been Too Wrapped Up

in things, new job, new books,
new paints for the canvas, to let
the thoughts go until they settle

on something startling: this world
for example, how it might be
otherwise if there were no colors,

if what came to us as the sea
were not blue, but a series of lines
you had to shape into swirling waves

to understand their essence.
I would cut fishline, tape it
to glass, then as a child might,

look through the surface
to the bottom. There would be Venice,
mosaic-goddess of the world,

found hundreds of years from now
at the bottom of the sea,
and in St. Mark's Square: a cathedral,

its walls and ceiling lined with stones,
faceted, ornamental stones in the shape
of Byzantine heroes. I would paint

the mosaics with water, let the Adriatic
Sea lap over their frosted surfaces.
On a day such as this, I do not need

to know colors to appreciate the property
of things. I can take a piece of string,
draw a basilica, look through its roof

to the inner walls where figures
touch one another and come to life
without the sun that lies

at the center of things
waiting to come to us
as coral, yellow, blue, or gold.

RON SMITH

PHOTOGRAPH OF JESSE OWENS AT THE GUN

Beneath a puff of white gun smoke a man
the shade of cinders has risen
from between white lines
at an angle sharp with speed.
He is himself a thrust of angles:
one foot down, one hand reaching,
elbow, knee, the single bend at the waist,
all his flesh strung tight.

In the background row of pale, blurred faces
these who appear to wear his colors
must be his teammates.
We can tell only that
they do not seem to cheer.
Behind them the tiers of Berlin
mass into gray clouds.

All the races of 1936 are stopped
inside this black frame.
The man whose captured body
pulls us to the wall
cannot reach the tape, his form
caught here in the rough shape
of the swastikas that fly in the corner.

Nothing moves, nothing changes.
We stare and stare.

This poem is dedicated to Dave Smith, T.R. Hummer, & Carolyn Kizer.

Sofia M. Starnes

The Monument Restorer

Between storms,
an obelisk, a man, and his oils
of a late sun, streaming. He toils
away in the heart-cavity
of a field. A yard or so

from our ankles,
he soft-brushes the dead.
Lion mane, luminous head;
hands, bristly as paws, tease up
the earth: five years in still

company.
   They're everywhere—
foot over flat foot, hair
wisp on hair, shoe buckle and
loosed linen: *Sheol. Sheol.*

Lord, how we bury, bless,
commend them to oak groans
and wonder: the universe owns.
   Could it be otherwise?
We, swallowing the world, it

and the withering stars,
the carbon dissolution of a place
so intended. Once out of the race—
we, with a brush on the bricks,
leveling ages.

   Sweethearts and weeds,
the man and his broom,
the obelisk and the small room
under, where no one lies,
sleeps, waits. I'd swear

a lost locket appears simply
from loving—gold in the crook
of his arm where dusk leaks. Look!
   Full are the man and the field,
   full are we under the sun.

The Poetry Society of Virginia
Centennial Anthology
Appendix A
The President

The president of The Poetry Society of Virginia (PSV) is the overall manager of this organization. As a group, poets tend to have grand ideals and ideas for how things should be, but it is up to the president to be pragmatic, to figure out which things can actually be done and, if so, how they can actually be accomplished.

The overall mission of the PSV is to promote the writing and enjoyment of poetry through a wide range of programs and monthly events. When the PSV was created 100 years ago, those "programs and monthly events" consisted of readings conducted in one central location. Since then, the PSV has expanded its contest to include nearly three dozen adult and student categories; has added a North American Book Award; has expanded its outreach to include workshops, in-school programs, poetry festivals, and other activities; and has broadened its readings and other poetry events to include venues throughout Virginia.

Today, the PSV is split up into seven regions across the state. Regional vice presidents manage the affairs of their individual regions, but their unified effort is also overseen and directed by the president. The president appoints chairpersons to various committees and coordinates with members of an executive board and elected officials in finance, membership, contests, and parliamentarian procedures.

The first president to bear the burden of this office was Dr. Charles N. Feidelson, who was voted into office in May 1923. When first conceived, the position was a one-year term and a president could serve no more than four years. Current bylaws have made the position a two-year term, but the four-year restriction still applies. Presidential duties as outlined in the PSV bylaws are listed here:

> It shall be the responsibility of the President/Chair of the Board, when present, to preside over all meetings of the Board of Directors and Executive Committee. The President/Chair of the Board is authorized to execute, in the name of the Society, any and all contracts or other documents which may be authorized, either generally or specifically, by the Board to be executed by the Society.

> It shall be the responsibility of the President, in general, to supervise and conduct all activities and operations of the Society, subject to the control, advice and consent of the Board of Directors. The President shall keep the Board of Directors completely informed, shall freely consult with them in relation to all activities of the Society, and shall see that all orders and/or resolutions of the Board are carried out to the effect intended.

> The President shall be empowered to act, speak for, or otherwise represent the Society between meetings of the Board. The President shall be responsible for the hiring and firing of all personnel (if any) excepting an Executive Director (if any), and shall be responsible for keeping the Board informed at all times of staff performance and for implementing any personnel policies which may be adopted and implemented by the Board.

The President, at all times, is authorized to contract on behalf of the Society and to execute in the name of the Society all contracts and other documents, authorized either generally or specifically by the Board to be executed by the PSV, and to negotiate any and all material business transactions of the Society. The President may sign checks for the Society if the Treasurer is unavailable.

The President is an ex officio member of all committees except the Nominating Committee, and serves as the principal representative of the Society.

But many situations arise that go beyond these bylaws, and the president must be agile enough to adjust to any fluid situation and guide the membership toward a beneficial solution. It is an arduous and all-encompassing burden.

Serving The Poetry Society of Virginia as president over its first one hundred years are thirty- eight member poets. Many have distinguished themselves through leadership in difficult times, as well as their skill with the written word. Their names are shown below:

Dr. C. E. Feidelson	Dr. Arthur Stocker	J. Ron Smith
Virginia Taylor McCormick	Dr. Roberta Cornelius	Tom Russell
Francis Macon	Harry Meacham	Edward W. Lull
Robert M. Hughes	Bess Gresham	Shirley N. Sellers
Virginia Lyne Tunstall	Louis Carlton	Patsy Anne Bickerstaff
Julia Johnson Davis	Dr. Keith Crim	Nancy Powell
Florence Dickenson Stearns	A. J. Mapp, Jr.	Judith Bragg
Emma Gray Trigg	Ellen Anderson	Guy Terrell
John Richard Moreland	Lorraine Smith	Robert Arthur
Brodie Herndon	Dr. Bruce Souders	Jeffrey Hewitt
Carleton Drewry	Dr. James McNally	Derek Kannemeyer
Barbara Whitney	Joseph Awad	Terry Cox-Joseph
Leslie Jones	J. Pendleton Campbell	

The Poetry Society of Virginia
Centennial Anthology
Appendix B
Poet Laureate of Virginia

Poet Laureate Of Virginia
Position History

The position of Poet Laureate of Virginia was first established on December 18, 1936.

Virginia Poets Laureate, from 1936 to 1996, before the position was codified by the General Assembly

Carter Warner Wormeley (1936 – 1938) was born in 1874. He was the advertising and publicity director for the Commonwealth of Virginia, as well as a Richmond journalist. In 1936 the Virginia General Assembly awarded him a lifetime appointment as poet laureate. He was the first such appointee in the history of the state. He passed away at the age of 64 and is buried in Hollywood Cemetery in Richmond.

From: *[POETS LAUREATE | Poetry Society (poetrysocietyofvirginia.org)]*

Charles Day (1942 – 1948). No biographical information about this poet laureate is currently available.

Thomas Lomax Hunter (1948), lawyer and poet, was born on March 6, 1875, in King George County, Virginia. After receiving his preliminary education with private tutors, he attended William and Mary and Georgetown University, where he studied law. Admitted to the bar of Virginia in 1908, he began to practice in King George and continued there until the close of his life. He was a frequent contributor to literary magazines and was best known as a poet. In 1948 he was named poet laureate by the Virginia General Assembly. His books include *Forbidden Fruit and Other Ballades* (East Aurora, 1923) and *Poems* (The Dietz Printing Co., 1947). He died in Fredericksburg, Virginia, on June 19, 1948.

From: *[Hunter, Thomas Lomax (lawlit.net)]*

Leigh Buckner Hanes (1949) was appointed to a one-year term as poet laureate by the Virginia General Assembly. He was the author of *Song of the New Hercules* (Four Seas Company, 1930) and contributed verse and reviews to magazines. He also wrote the words for songs, including "Mountains," "Love Shall Light the Haven," and "Mountains in Twilight." He died in Roanoke, Virginia, in 1967, at the age of 73.

From: *[https://www.findagrave.com/memorial/8464762/leigh-buckner-hanes]*

Ruby Altizer Roberts (1950; appointed Poet Laureate Emerita in 1992) was the author of two collections of poetry, *Forever Is Too Long* (Wings Press, 1946) and *Command the Stars* (Wings Press, 1948). She also authored three memoirs, a children's book, and a genealogical history. She was named Virginia's first female poet laureate in 1950 and until 1994 was the only woman to have held the post. In addition, Roberts edited the poetry journal *The Lyric* from 1952 to 1977. In 1961 she received an honorary Doctor of Humanities degree from William and Mary in Williamsburg, and in 1992, the General Assembly designated her Poet Laureate Emerita of Virginia. She was born in 1907 and passed away in 2004.

From: [Ruby Altizer Roberts (1907–2004) – Encyclopedia Virginia]

Guy Carleton Drewry (1970 – 1991), the author of six poetry books, was born in Franklin County, Virginia, in 1901 and served a lifetime appointment as poet laureate. Although he had no formal education, his sister taught him how to read, and he practiced poetry through hymnals. Drewry served as associate editor of *The Lyric* and published in *Virginia Quarterly Review, Yale Review, Poetry, The Dial, The New York Times* and *The Nation*. After retiring from his statistician position in 1966, he devoted his time to poetry and served as President of the Virginia Poetry Society and as a Regional Vice-President of the Poetry Society of America. His awards include a Keats Memorial Lyric Prize and a Foundation Prize for Best Volume of Poems in English for *A Time for Turning* (E. P. Dutton & Company, 1951).

From: [https://en.wikipedia.org/wiki/Guy_Carleton_Drewry]

Kathryn Forrester Thro (1994 – 1996) is an artist, playwright, and author of seven books, including *Laurel the Flower Girl* and *Three Cats at a Wedding*, her first children's rhyming picture book, as well as *Mary's Joy, A Dance with Angels* (CreateSpace Independent Publishing). She is foundress of *Mary's Joy*, a helping-hands ministry "linking those in need with those who can help." Her campaign "Anti-Violence through the Medium of Poetry" was recognized by then-Governor George Allen. She has traveled to schools and universities with a message of hope for youths affected by poverty, gang violence, and peer pressure. The focus of her poetry has been on Virginia's heritage, and she has shared her unique perceptions of Virginia history and Virginia's great historical figures.

From: [http://marysjoy.blogspot.com]
     [https://www.linkedin.com/in/kathryn-forrester-thro-obl-s-b-50924697]
     [https://lis.virginia.gov/cgi-bin/legp604.exe?941+ful+HJ58+pdf]

Codification of the Virginia Poet Laureate position in 1998
Virginia Code, § 1-512.

The honorary position of Poet Laureate of Virginia is hereby created. Beginning in 1998, the Governor may appoint a poet laureate from a list of nominees submitted by The Poetry Society of Virginia. Each poet laureate shall serve a term of two years with no restrictions on reappointment.

From: *[https://law.lis.virginia.gov/vacode/title1/chapter5/section1-512/]*

Virginia Poets Laureate from 1996 – 2022

Margaret Ward Morland (1996 – 1998) Born in Birmingham, Alabama, in 1923, Margaret Ward Morland graduated with highest honors from Samford University and received an M.A. in English at the University of North Carolina, Chapel Hill. She published two volumes of poetry, *It Happens Thus* (Bargara Press, 1983) and *Gift of Jade* (Forest Woods Media Production, 1998). Individual poems have appeared widely in periodicals and anthologies, including *The Christian Science Monitor, Blue Unicorn,* and *Poets for Africa: An International Anthology for Hunger Relief.* Her work received the Arts Award of the Academy of Women, Cecil Hackney Award from Birmingham-Southern College, Conrad Aiken Prize from the Poetry Society of Georgia, National Lutheran Hymn Prize, and the Nancy Byrd Turner Prize from The Poetry Society of Virginia, and she was recognized with a Distinguished Alumna Award from Samford University.

Morland's poems have been featured in juried exhibitions with paintings, sculpture, and photography. More than sixty poems have been set to music and performed by choirs and choruses from Bruton Parish Church in Williamsburg to the University of Alaska, Fairbanks. She taught at Samford University and Lynchburg College and gave readings and workshops in the United States, Europe, Hong Kong, Taiwan, and mainland China.

From: *[Kreiter-Foronda and Lull, Eds. Four Virginia Poets Laureate: A Teaching Guide. The Poetry Society of Virginia, ©2006.]*
[https: digitalcommons.odu.edu/virginiapoets/westcentral/poets/4/]
[https:encyclopediavirginia.org/interview-with-margaret-ward-morland-2/]

Joseph Awad (1998 – 2000) Born in Shenandoah, Pennsylvania, during the Great Depression, Joseph Awad (May 17, 1929 – July 17, 2009) grew up in Washington, DC. He received his baccalaureate degree in English from Georgetown University, where he edited the *Georgetown Journal* and graduated cum laude. He completed his graduate work in English at George Washington University. After working part time for the Washington bureau of the New York *Daily News,* he began a career in public relations. He joined Reynolds Metals Company in 1957 and retired as Vice President in 1993. His stature in the public relations field led to his election as national president of the Public Relations

Society of America, and the first elected chairman of its College of Fellows. After publishing his book *The Power of Public Relations* (Praeger, 1985) he was named to Virginia's Communications Hall of Fame.

Although he began writing poetry as a teenager, his first book of poetry, *The Neon Distances* was not published until 1989 (MacMillan Publishing Company). The second, *Shenandoah Long Ago* (Poet's Press, 1990) contains vivid memories of his childhood in Shenandoah. *The Big Bang*, a long poem in twelve cantos, was published in its entirety in the *Edge City Review*, and as a book in 1999 (The Poet's Press). *Leaning to Hear the Music* appeared in 1997 (Road Publishers). Individual poems have been featured in *America, Kansas Quarterly, The William & Mary Review, Commonweal, The Hollins Critic, The Formalist, The Lyric*, and many other journals. His poem "Autumnal" appeared in the college text book *Approaching Literature in the 21ˢᵗ Century*. His poetry won *The Lyric*'s Nathan Haskell Dole Prize, the Donn Goodwin Poetry Award, and the Edgar Allan Poe Prize of The Poetry Society of Virginia. Awad was a former President of The Poetry Society of Virginia and Vice-President of the Virginia Writers Club.

From: *[Kreiter-Foronda and Lull, Eds. Four Virginia Poets Laureate: A Teaching Guide. The Poetry Society of Virginia, ©2006.]*
[https://en.wikipedia.org/wiki/Joseph_Awad]

Grace Pow Simpson (2000 – 2002) A native of South Carolina, Grace Pow Simpson (September 16, 1931 – February 11, 2016) earned a bachelor's degree from Winthrop College and an MA in English from Longwood College. She taught at Longwood, Florida State University, Auburn University, and was a teacher of English, creative writing, and journalism at Prince Edward County High School for fifteen years. An advocate of poetry and a member of The Poetry Society of Virginia, she published widely in such journals as *The Cincinnati Poetry Review, The Formalist, Southern Poetry Review*, and *Zone 3*, from which she received the Rainmaker Award in 1991. Virginia Governor Jim Gilmore appointed Simpson as Virginia Poet Laureate for 2000 – 2002. During her term she traveled across the state, giving readings and talks. She stressed that verse should be memorized so that it is immediately available as a comfort or a pleasure. Her collection *Dancing the Bones* won the Writer's Digest award for the best self-published poetry book of 2001. That year, she read from her work at the National Festival of the Book in Washington, D.C. In 2002, Hampden-Sydney College awarded her an honorary Doctorate of Humane Letters, and in 2008 she was featured at the Virginia Festival of the Book with Poets Laureate Emerita Margaret Ward Morland, Joseph Awad, a representative of George Garrett, and then-Poet Laureate Carolyn Kreiter-Foronda.

From: *[Kreiter-Foronda and Lull, Eds. Four Virginia Poets Laureate: A Teaching Guide. The Poetry Society of Virginia, ©2006.]*
[www.farmvilleherald.com/2016/02/grace-pow-simpson/]

George Garrett (2002 – 2004) Author of more than 30 books of fiction, poetry, biography and criticism, George Garrett (June 11, 1929 – May 25, 2008) was the Henry Hoyns Professor of Creative Writing at the University of Virginia. He also held adjunct or short-term positions at nearly a dozen schools, including Wesleyan University, Bennington College, Princeton University and the Virginia Military Institute. He was Contemporary Poetry Series editor at the University of North Carolina Press, Chapel Hill, a United States poetry editor for *Transatlantic Review*, and co-editor of *Hollins Critic*. Garrett earned his BA, MA, and PhD. degrees from Princeton University. Among his honors and awards were fellowships from the Guggenheim, Ford, and Rockefeller Foundations, a *Sewanee Review* Fellowship in Poetry, as well as the National Endowment for the Arts Fellowship. Dr. Garrett received the T. S. Eliot Award of the Ingersoll Foundation, the Aiken Taylor Award for Modern American Poetry, the PEN/Malamud Award for Excellence in Short Fiction, the Commonwealth of Virginia Governor's Award for the Arts, and an Award in Literature from the American Academy of Arts and Letters. He also received the Hollins Medal and an honorary degree from the University of the South and was the recipient of the 2005 Cleanth Brooks Medal for Distinguished Achievement in Southern Letters.

From: *[Kreiter-Foronda and Lull, Eds. Four Virginia Poets Laureate: A Teaching Guide. The Poetry Society of Virginia, ©2006.]*
[https://www.poetryfoundation.org/poets/george-garrett]
[https://en.wikipedia.org/wiki/George_Garrett_(poet)]

Rita Dove (2004 – 2006) Rita Dove is a Pulitzer Prize winning American poet and writer, who served as Poet Laureate of the United States from 1993 – 1995 and as Poet Laureate of Virginia from 2004 – 2006. In her public posts, Dove concentrated on spreading the word about poetry and increasing public awareness of the benefits of literature. As United States Poet Laureate, she brought together writers to explore the African diaspora through the eyes of its artists. In 1973 she graduated summa cum laude from Miami University and received an M.F.A. from the University of Iowa in 1977.

Dove has authored numerous books, including *Playlist for the Apocalypse*, published by W. W. Norton in August 2021. The recipient of 28 honorary doctorates from a range of universities, Dove has won many awards, including the Wallace Stevens Award from the Academy of American Poets, the Kenyon Review Award for Literary Achievement, Cleveland Arts Prize for Lifetime Achievement, Virginia Commission for the Arts "50 for 50 Arts Inspiration Award," NAACP Image Award for Outstanding Literary Work for *Collected Poems: 1974 – 2004*, the Harold Washington Literary Award, the U.S. Presidential Scholars Award, the Stone Award for Lifetime Achievement, the Poetry and People International Prize (Guangdong, China), Carole Weinstein Prize, Women of Achievement Award, National Medal of Arts, Fulbright Lifetime Achievement Medal, Library of Virginia Lifetime Achievement Award, Common Wealth Award of Distinguished Service, and Charles Frankel Prize (National Humanities Medal).

An acclaimed lyricist, Dove has written lyrics for composers ranging from

Tania León to John Williams. In 2001 the popular *Thomas and Beulah* (Carnegie Mellon Press, 1986) was staged as an opera by the Museum for Contemporary Art in Chicago. Dove is currently the Henry Hoyns Professor of Creative Writing at the University of Virginia. In 2021 she received the Gold Medal in poetry from the American Academy of Arts and Letters, the Academy's highest honor.

From: *[https://poets.org/poet/rita-dove]*
            [https://www.biography.com/writer/rita-dove]
            [Starnes, Sofia, Ed. Four Virginia Poets Laureate: An Anthology and Reader's Guide, Cedar Creek Publishing, ©2013.]

Carolyn Kreiter-Foronda (2006 – 2008) Carolyn Kreiter-Foronda has published ten books of poetry, co-edited four anthologies and co-authored a poem-play. She holds a B.A. from the University of Mary Washington (Mortar Board; Phi Beta Kappa) and advanced degrees from George Mason University, where she received the university's first doctorate, an Outstanding Academic Achievement and Service Award, and a Letter of Recognition for Quality Research from Virginia Educational Research Association for her dissertation, *Gathering Light: A Poet's Approach to Poetry Analysis*. In 2007 both universities gave her the Distinguished Alumna of the Year Award. She has received five grants from the Virginia Commission for the Arts and has won the international Art-in-Literature: The Mary Lynn Kotz Award, the Ellen Anderson Award, Virginia Cultural Laureate Award, an Edgar Allan Poe Poetry Award, six Pushcart Prize nominations, as well as other awards.

During her tenure as Poet Laureate of Virginia, Dr. Foronda conducted numerous workshops at schools and universities throughout the Commonwealth as part of the Poetry-in-the-Schools Program, which she established in 2001 at the request of The Poetry Society of Virginia. She initiated and led the effort to fund five Academy of American Poets Endowed Poetry Prizes at Virginia Tech, William and Mary, University of Richmond, University of Mary Washington, and Old Dominion University. She established a Poetry Book Giveaway Project, co-edited *Four Virginia Poets Laureate: A Teaching Guide* (The Poetry Society of Virginia, 2006), wrote *River Country* to promote the ecosystem of the Tidewater region, set up a Poet's Spotlight feature on her website to promote poets of all races and ages, judged Poetry Out Loud competitions, and participated in activities highlighting Hispanic poets and poetry at the Library of Congress. In addition, she took part in state poets laureate events in New Hampshire, Rhode Island, Indiana, South Carolina, Tennessee, Washington, DC, Kansas, and Maryland. For her dedicated service as poet laureate, she received a resolution of appreciation from the Virginia Board of Education.

From: *[www.carolynforonda.com]*
            [https://www.pw.org/directory/writers/carolyn_kreiterforonda]
            [https://en.wikipedia.org/wiki/Carolyn_Kreiter-Foronda]
            [Starnes, Sofia, Ed. Four Virginia Poets Laureate: An Anthology and Reader's Guide, Cedar Creek Publishing, ©2013.]

Claudia Emerson (2008 – 2010) Born and raised in Chatham, Virginia, Claudia Emerson (January 13, 1957 – December 4, 2014) received a B.A. from the University of Virginia and an M.F.A. from the University of North Carolina, where she served as poetry editor for the *Greensboro Review*. She taught at Washington and Lee University, Randolph-Macon Women's College, the University of Mary Washington, and Virginia Commonwealth University. She received numerous awards, including the Pulitzer Prize for *Late Wife* (LSU Press, 2005), fellowships from the Library of Congress, the Virginia Commission for the Arts, and the National Endowment for the Arts. She also won the Erskine J. Poetry Prize from *Smartish Pace* (2004), the University of Mary Washington Mary Pinschmidt Teaching Award (2006), the Carole Weinstein Poetry Award (2007), among other recognitions. She was the author of eight poetry collections.

During her term as Poet Laureate of Virginia, Emerson served as a Literary Arts Specialist for the DC Metrorail Public Art in Transit Project, which highlights poems by former Virginia Poets Laureate, as well as by established and emerging poets. She was selected by the Library of Virginia as a "Virginia Woman in History" and served on the jury for the state's Poetry Out Loud Contest. In addition, she gave readings and/or presentations at numerous sites, including Old Dominion University, Vanderbilt, University of North Carolina, Spalding University, and Folger Shakespeare Library.

From: *[https://en.wikipedia.org/wiki/Claudia_Emerson]*
[https:www.poetryfoundation.org/poets/claudia-emerson]
[https://poets.org/poet/claudia-emerson]
[Starnes, Sofia, Ed. Four Virginia Poets Laureate: An Anthology and Reader's Guide, Cedar Creek Publishing, ©2013.]

Kelly Cherry (2010 – 2012) Kelly Cherry (1940-2022), was born in Baton Rouge, Louisiana, but spent most of her childhood and early adulthood in Richmond, Virginia. She died in Halifax, Virginia, in 2022. The author of 27 books of poetry, fiction, and nonfiction, she also authored 11 chapbooks and translated two classical plays. In 1961 she graduated from the University of Mary Washington and received the Distinguished Alumnus Award from UMW in 2000. She completed graduate work at the University of Virginia as a Du Pont Fellow and received a Masters of Fine Arts from the University of North Carolina in Greensboro. For over 20 years she taught at the University of Wisconsin-Madison. Cherry received fellowships from the Rockefeller Foundation, the National Endowment for the Arts, the Ragdale Foundation, and Yaddo. She also was the inaugural recipient of both the Hanes Award for Poetry from the Fellowship of Southern Writers and the Ellen Anderson Award. She received a Lifetime Achievement Award from UNC at Greensboro, the L.E. Phillabaum Poetry Award, and the Carole Weinstein Poetry Prize.

In July, 2010, Cherry was named Virginia Poet Laureate by Governor Bob McDonnell. During her tenure, she focused on bringing poetry to the many retirement communities and rehabilitation centers in the Commonwealth.

From: *[https://www.poetryfoundation.org/poets/kelly-cherry]*
[https://poets.org/poet/kelly-cherry]

[*https:www.pw.org/directory/writers/kelly_cherry*]
[*Starnes, Sofia, Ed. Four Virginia Poets Laureate: An Anthology and Reader's Guide, Cedar Creek Publishing, ©2013.*]

Sofia M. Starnes (2012 – 2014) Sofia M. Starnes is a writer of Philippine-Spanish heritage, who has been an American citizen since 1989. She received an advanced degree in English Philology from the University of Madrid, and holds a degree in English Pedagogy from the Instituto de Idiomas in Madrid. Starnes is the author of six poetry collections, including *The Consequence of Moonlight* (Paraclete Press, 2018). She is the recipient of a Poetry Fellowship from the Virginia Commission for the Arts, co-winner of the 2001 Aldrich Poetry Prize, recipient of the Rainer Maria Rilke Poetry Prize, the Whitebird Poetry Series Prize, five Pushcart Prize nominations, an Editor's Prize in the 2001 Transcontinental Poetry Award competition, an honorary Doctor of Letters degree from Union College, Kentucky, among other awards. Starnes's poetry has appeared in numerous journals, including *Poetry, Hayden's Ferry Review, Gulf Coast, Modern Age, Southern Poetry Review, Notre Dame Review, Hubbub, Pleiades, Madison Review,* and *Bellevue Literary Review.*

During her tenure as poet laureate, Starnes's goal was to encourage the reading of poetry by affirming the centrality of the reader in the fulfillment of any poem. She contends that poetry does not thrive if it is read only by poets. To this end, she edited *The Nearest Poem Anthology* (Cedar Creek Press, 2014), which includes over 100 poems, each with a short essay explaining why the poem is meaningful to that reader. The poems range from classic to contemporary, and reflect different cultural and linguistic traditions. One major state university selected the book as a graduation present for its seniors. In addition, during her term Starnes was a guest presenter at the Highlands Festival in Abingdon, the Patrick Hayes Writers Series at William and Mary, the VATE Annual Conference, Virginia Tech, the Prince William County Arts Event, the James River Writers Conference, the National League of American Pen Women Biennial Celebration, the Virginia Festival of the Book, Patrick Henry College, Franciscan University in Steubenville, Ohio, Michigan State University, as well as other locations statewide and beyond.

From: [*sofiamstarnes.com*]
           [*https//www.poetryfoundation.org/poets/sofia-starnes*]
           [*https//www.pw.org/directory/writers/sofia_m_starnes*]

Ron Smith (2014 – 2016) Ron Smith is the first writer-in-residence at St. Christopher's School in Richmond, Virginia. The author of five books of poetry, he has won numerous awards, including the Carole Weinstein Poetry Prize, the Ellen Anderson Award, *Southern Poetry Review's* Guy Owen Prize, and *Poetry Northwest's* Theodore Roethke Prize. His poems have appeared in *The Nation, Kenyon Review, New England Review* and in anthologies from Wesleyan University Press, Time-Life Books, University of Virginia Press, University of Georgia Press, and University of Illinois Press. He has served as President of The Poetry Society of Virginia, as Vice President of the Board of Trustees of the Edgar Allan Poe Museum, and as a Trustee for James River Writers. Since 2010, he has served as

Poetry Editor of *Aethlon: The Journal of Sport Literature*.

During his term as Poet Laureate of Virginia, Smith launched a blog spotlighting, promoting, and encouraging poets in the Commonwealth, as well as a poetry column interacting with readers of *Shenandoah*. As his invocation on the floor of the Virginia Senate, Smith read his poem "Angelus: Chesapeake Bay," and as his invocation on the floor of the Virginia House of Delegates, Smith read his poem "Suitor," about George and Martha Washington. He read his poems about Thomas Jefferson at Monticello. At Mount Vernon, he organized "Tea & Fellowship with the Poet Laureate of Virginia," an event that included three previous Virginia Poets Laureate: Kelly Cherry, Sofia Starnes, and Carolyn Kreiter-Foronda. In addition, Smith carried Virginia's poetry abroad. From British Columbia to Dublin, Ireland, to the Italian Alps, to the Keats-Shelley House and the official U.S. Ambassador's Residence in Rome, he shared his love of the Commonwealth through readings and presentations.

From: [*https://en.wikipedia.org/wiki/Ron_Smith_(American_poet)*]
[*https://vapoetlaureate.wordpress.com/about/*]

Tim Seibles (2016 – 2018) Tim Seibles is an American poet and educator. He earned a B.A. at Southern Methodist University and an M.F.A. at Vermont College of Norwich University. He is the author of nine poetry collections, including *Voodoo Libretto: New & Selected Poems* (Etruscan Press, 2022), *One Turn Around the Sun* (Etruscan Press, 2017), *Body Moves* (Carnegie Mellon Press, 2013), *Buffalo Head Solos* (Cleveland State University Press, 2004), *Hammerlock* (Cleveland State University Press, 1999), and *Fast Animal* (Etruscan Press, 2012), which won the Theodore Roethke Memorial Poetry Prize, the PEN Oakland Josephine Miles Award, and was named a finalist for a National Book Award.

Seibles carries the distinction of being the first African-American man to serve as Virginia Poet Laureate. His honors include an Open Voice Award and fellowships from the National Endowment for the Arts and the Provincetown Fine Arts Work Center. His poems have been published in numerous literary journals and magazines including *Callaloo*, *The Kenyon Review*, *Indiana Review*, *Ploughshares*, *Rattle*, and in the anthologies *Verse & Universe: Poems about Science and Mathematics* (Milkweed Editions, 1998) and *New American Poets in the 90's* (David R. Godine, 1991). He has taught at Old Dominion University, the University of Southern Maine's Stonecoast M.F.A. program, and has led workshops at Cave Canem.

From: [*https://www.poetryfoundation.org/poets/tim-seibles*]
[*https://poets.org/poet/tim-seibles*]
[*https://en.wikipedia.org/wiki/tim_seibles*]

Henry Hart (2018 – 2020) Henry Hart grew up on a small Christmas tree farm in New England and began studying and writing poetry when he attended Dartmouth College in 1972. He continued to write poetry at Oxford University, where he received a doctorate in 1983. While in England, Dr. Hart and two Scottish friends established the international poetry journal *Verse*, which he helped edit for two decades. He has published four books of poetry, and in 2010 was awarded Virginia's Carole Weinstein Poetry Prize. He has also published scholarly books on Robert Lowell, Seamus Heaney, and Geoffrey Hill. His biography of James Dickey was a runner-up for a Southern Book Critics' Circle Award in 2000. His biography, *The Life of Robert Frost,* was published by Wiley-Blackwell in 2017. Dr. Hart has taught English for over three decades at the College of William and Mary, where he is currently the Mildred and J.B. Hickman Professor of Humanities.

During his term as Virginia Poet Laureate, Dr. Hart worked on fundraising projects for The Poetry Society of Virginia. He secured substantial donations, as well as a permanent location at William and Mary for the Society's annual poetry festival. He hopes this financial assistance from Anne Willis and the former William and Mary President Paul Verkuil will keep the PSV on a solid foundation for years to come.

From: *[https://www.wm.edu/news/stories/2018/henry-hart-has-a-new-title-poet-laureate-of-virginia.php]*
[https://en.wikipedia.org/wiki/henry_hart_(author)]

Luisa A. Igloria (2020 – 2022) Originally from Baguio City, the Philippines, Luisa A. Igloria is the author of *Maps for Migrants and Ghosts* (Co-Winner, 2019 Crab Orchard Open Poetry Prize, Southern Illinois University Press, 2020), *The Buddha Wonders if She is Having a Mid-Life Crisis* (Phoenicia Publishing, Montreal, 2018), and 12 other books. Igloria was the inaugural recipient of the 2015 Resurgence Poetry Prize (UK) for ecopoetry and is a Louis I. Jaffe Professor of English and Creative Writing in the M.F.A. Program at Old Dominion University. She also leads workshops for The Muse Writers Center in Norfolk.

Gov. Ralph Northam invited Dr. Igloria to read poetry for the 2021 Juneteenth Program at historic Old Point Comfort, Hampton, Virginia. She has been featured on National Public Radio and has served in regional, state, and national forums as panelist, literary competition judge, and/or keynote speaker/ poetry reader/workshop leader. In 2021, Dr. Igloria spearheaded the creation of two solidarity programs: one, a conversation panel with AAPI (Asian American and Pacific Islander) community leaders and ODU alumni; and the other, the "Stronger Together" solidarity reading she coordinated with AAPI faculty and students from across the university, who read poems and shared their concerns about the growing violence against AAPIs.

In 2021, Dr. Igloria was one of 23 recipients nationwide of a Poet Laureate Fellowship from the Academy of American Poets and the Mellon Foundation. Her public poetry projects for this fellowship included designing and launching a Young Poets in the Community program, a Virginia Poets Database (permanently housed through Old Dominion University's digital commons platform), and a year of poetry readings and panel conversations.

From: *[https://www.odu.edu/directory/people/l/igloria]*
[www.luisaigloria.com]
[https://www.loc.gov/rr/main/poets/Virginia.html]

The Poetry Society of Virginia
Centennial Anthology
Appendix C
Meet the Poets

Obelia Akanke has published several short stories, novellas, and novels. Drawing from her education and experience in social services, she often includes messages or lessons to bring awareness to a situation and to help the reader grow in compassion and understanding for others.

Angela Anselmo joined The Poetry Society of Virginia in 2000. She has since published two books of poetry. In her words, writing poetry is a journey. You begin with a destination in mind, but as you write, the poem often takes you somewhere else, making it a magical and enriching experience.

April J. Asbury earned her M.F.A. from Spalding University and M.A. from Hollins. She teaches writing at Radford. Her work appears in *Artemis, Still: The Journal, The Anthology of Appalachian Writers,* and other publications. In 2021, Finishing Line Press published her poetry collection *Woman With Crows.*

Bill Ayres has worked running or helping to run bookstores since the invention of ink. His work has appeared in *Commonweal, Sojourners, The Hollins Critic, Hoot, The Roanoke Review, Antietam Review,* and other journals. He is the author of *What Passes For Wisdom* (Finishing Line Press, 2020).

Zeina Azzam is a Palestinian American poet, editor, and community activist. Her poems appear in over forty literary journals and anthologies, and her chapbook *Bayna, Bayna In-Between* was published by Poetry Box in 2021. She holds M.A. degrees in Arabic Literature from Georgetown University and in Sociology from George Mason University.

Madalin Jackson Bickel, a graduate of Marshall University with both B.A. and M.A. degrees, has published two collections of poetry and three cozy mysteries, as well as individual poems in numerous anthologies. She belongs to Riverside Writers, Virginia Writers, and West Virginia Writers, in addition to The Poetry Society of Virginia.

Patsy Anne Bickerstaff, B.A., J.D. (UR), Bread Loaf Conference Participant, was a PSV member since 1964 and held various offices, including that of president (four terms). Winner of the 1985 Robert Penn Warren Prize, she published over 300 poems, four books, and wrote a poetry column, The Cloak, for St. Martin's Church, Richmond. She passed away on January 11, 2023.

Dry wit and a touch of wisdom characterize the poems of humorist **Laura J. Bobrow.** A nonagenarian, Laura is a professional storyteller as well. More than 100 of her poems have appeared over the years in various media, including a fourth-grade textbook in Abu Dhabi.

Jim Boucher of Burke, Virginia, worked thirty years in the pension field and fifteen years at a library in Manassas, Virginia. A notable duty there was to write captions for the library entrance, such as, "Choose a book, no need to pay; just return it by its due day."

Jack Callan sits out in the cold night and writes poetry, sits with wild animals and doesn't get eaten, endures weather extremes with great interest, and will go so far as to read his first draft to white tail deer come down at evenin' who hiss their disapproval. (He promises to edit and does.) He reads the final draft at The Little River Poetry Festival each June, in that there field.

Joan Ellen Casey started writing poetry at age twelve and never stopped through various careers, world travels, and life events. After completing a doctorate at William and Mary, she continued taking courses and designing educational programs. Joan is an award-winning poet and has been published in a dozen anthologies.

Kenneth F. Conklin, a native of Los Angeles, has lived in Botetourt County since 2005. His essays appear in the *Roanoke Times* and other publications. *NORVEL: an American Hero* (2020) was his debut book. His book of poems *The Zen of Ken* was published in 2021.

Terry Cox-Joseph, poet, artist, former newspaper reporter and editor, was elected President of the Poetry Society of Virginia in 2021. Her poems have appeared widely, and her art has been on display in numerous galleries. Her poetry collection *Between Then and Now* was published by Finishing Line Press in 2018.

Kathleen P. Decker's poetry books include *Russian Reverie, Whispers on Paper, Essence of Woman,* and *Updraft.* She edited and published an international haiku journal, *Chiyo's Corner,* and was an editor for the World Haiku Association. She has edited three anthologies, *My Neighbor's Life, On Crimson Wings,* and *Quilted Poems.*

Pamela Brothers Denyes's award-winning poems appear in many journals and international collections. Her first books, *The Right Mistakes* and *The Widow's Lovers,* were published in 2022. Pamela's career-based writing included contract nonfiction, developmental editing, and online/print writing. Now retired, she's harvesting 40 years of poetry journals to create new works—and fun!

Sharon Canfield Dorsey, an award-winning poet and author, publishes fiction, nonfiction, juvenile fiction, and poetry in magazines, journals, and anthologies. She has also published four children's books, three poetry books, a memoir, and a travel journal. She served one term as vice-president for the Eastern Region, The Poetry Society of Virginia.

Linda Ankrah-Dove earned her M.F.A. in 2021. Her book, *Borrowed Glint of Jade* (2019), was followed by the publication of poems in over a dozen journals and anthologies. Her second book is currently out for publication, and a third is underway.

Angela (Angie) Dribben is an autistic Appalachian artist and writer. Her debut selection, *Everygirl,* finalist for the 2020 Broadkill Review Dogfish Head Prize, was released by *Main Street Rag.* Her most recent work can be found or is forthcoming in *Los Angeles Review, Orion, Coffin Bell, Split Rock Review,* and other publications.

John L. Dutton II has taught language arts to middle school students in Prince William County for more years than he can remember. He hosts *Spilled Ink VA,* an open microphone night celebrating the written word. He has published three books: *Armadillo Lost Her Pillow, Argument at the Airport,* and *Billy Pug's Bad Day.*

Anne Emerson lived in Northern Virginia for thirty-seven years before retiring with her husband to Williamsburg, Virginia. She enjoys gardening, observing human nature, and engaging in a variety of hobbies. Her poems have been published in *NoVA Bards* and *The Poets Domain.*

L. Nelson Farley has written humorous and satirical work, as well as both religious and worldly poems. He worked as a mechanical engineer, and for forty years gave away toys, ghost stories, and almonds to children and their families at Halloween. His planes and trains are now on display in museums.

Maurice Ferguson worked as the literary editor of *Artemis Journal* from 1980 until his retirement in 2021. His work has appeared or is forthcoming in *Artemis Journal, Inlet* (Wesleyan Press), *Forward Magazine, Sow's Ear, Virginia Quarterly, Piedmont Literary Review, Roanoke Review, Gargoyle Journal,* and numerous other publications.

Catherine Fletcher is a writer based in Norfolk, Virginia. Her recent work has appeared in *The Inflectionist Review, New World Writing, The Hopper, Hopkins Review,* and the concert series *Concept Lab.* She has received fellowships from the Virginia Commission for the Arts, Arizona State University, Brooklyn Arts Council, and other organizations.

Rich Follett is the Poet Laureate of Strasburg, VA. He has published four collections of poetry: *Responsorials* (2009), *Silence, Inhabited* (2011), and *Human & c.* (2013) through NeoPoesis Press, and an ekphrastic collection, *Photo-Ku* (2016), through NightWing Publications. Rich is featured in the Virginia Poets Database through ODU.

Eric J. Forsbergh won the Edgar Allan Poe Memorial Prize in 2013 and 2014. He has been published in *JAMA, Artemis, Streetlight, The Northern Virginia Review,* and other journals. A Navy Vietnam veteran and retired dentist, he was recently a volunteer COVID vaccinator, and attended seminary on social justice.

Chapman Hood Frazier's *The Lost Books of the Bestiary* was published in spring, 2022. A Professor in Residence for JMU, he completed a Ph.D. from UVA, was the Associate Director of the Young Writers Workshop, and Poetry Editor for Longwood University's *Dos Passos Review.* He lives in Rice with his wife Deborah Carrington.

Greg Friedmann has lived alongside a channel of the Potomac River in Northern Virginia for the last 35 years. His poetry has appeared in a variety of journals and often touches on riparian themes.

Sue Davis Gabbay has published three books of her poetry, and several of her stories have appeared in children's magazines. She holds a B.A. from Indiana University and an M.L.S. from Syracuse University.

James F. Gaines, past president of Riverside Writers of Fredericksburg, has published a collection of his Louisiana poems, *Downriver Waltz* (Amazon, 2021), and a volume of short fiction, *Beyond the Covenant and Other Stories* (Amazon, 2018). With his son John, he publishes the *Foriani Saga* of science fiction novels (Amazon, 2016, 2017, and forthcoming).

Stan Galloway founded the Bridgewater International Poetry Festival in 2013 and Pier-Glass Poetry in 2021. He has published, co-authored, or edited nine books and chapbooks. His work has been nominated for Best of the Net and Pushcart prizes. He has taught college English in the Shenandoah Valley since 1993.

Adele Gardner and her father/namesake **Delbert R. Gardner** have published over 425 poems in *American Arts Quarterly, Hollins Critic,* and other journals. Librarian Adele's poetry collection *Halloween Hearts* is forthcoming from Jackanapes Press. English professor/editor Delbert wrote *An "Idle Singer"and his Audience:A Study of William Morris's Poetic Reputation in England,1858-1900.*

James L. Garrett is a retired high school English teacher. He earned a B.A. from LaGrange College and is a Marine Corps veteran. He is a member of the James City Poets.

Claudia Gary, an internationally anthologized poet, teaches workshops on Villanelle, Sonnet, Natural Meter, and other poetic forms. She is the author of *Humor Me* (2006) and several chapbooks including *Genetic Revisionism* (2019). She is also a health/science journalist, a visual artist, and a composer of songs and chamber music.

Bill Glose, combat veteran and former paratrooper, is the author of five books of poetry. His latest collection, *Postscript to War,* was a finalist for the Library of Virginia Book Award. Glose was named *Daily Press* Poet Laureate in 2011 and featured by NPR on *The Writer's Almanac* in 2017.

June Goodenough, aka Ricci, has been published in small press poetry anthologies, military base newspapers, and *The Alcona County Review.* She earned her Mansfield State College English B.A. and is an Air Force retiree, an equestrian, and a Black Belt. She has also shot a bullseye 'Robin Hood' at 50 yards.

Katherine Gotthardt, an award-winning poet and author, believes in the power of writing to transform lives. She uses proceeds from her books to support nonprofit and community initiatives. When she is not writing or volunteering, she enjoys time with her husband, her grown children, and her rescue animals.

Marjorie Gowdy's chapbook *Inflorescence: The Pasture at Rest,* will be published in 2023 by Finishing Line Press. Her poems appear in such journals as *Clinch River Review, Artemis,* and *Roanoke Review,* and two of her poems are included in the anthology *Quilted Poems.* She earned a B.A. from VT and an M.A.L.S. from UNCG.

Lyman Grant lives in Harrisonburg, Virginia. He taught at Austin Community College for 44 years, where he also served as Dean of Arts and Humanities. His volumes of poems include *The Road Home* (Dalton, 2006), *As Long As We Need* (Black Buzzard Press, 2011), and *Old Men on Tuesday Mornings* (Alamo Bay Press, 2017).

David Habib's work has appeared in *The Virginia Normal, Whistling Shade,* and *New American Writing,* among other publications. Both a writer and a photographer, he lives in rural Loudoun County, Virginia.

Alexandra "Zan" Delaine Hailey (1992-2018) was an inaugural poet laureate in Prince William County, 2014-2016. Her writing has been published in *The Northern Virginia Review, Written in Arlington,* Virginia Commonwealth University's *Focused Inquiry* Textbook, *Bristow Beat,* and *New Departures Anthology.* Her chapbook *Intrastate Lines* is forthcoming from Finishing Line Press.

Cathy Hailey teaches in JHU's M.A. in Teaching Writing program and previously taught high school English and Creative Writing. She is Northern Region Vice-President of The Poetry Society of Virginia and organizes In the Company of Laureates, a poetry reading event. Her chapbook, *I'd Rather Be a Hyacinth,* is forthcoming from Finishing Line Press.

Mary Mallek Haines, a writer of Polish ancestry and author of *Beads of an Abacus* (San Francisco Bay Press, 2011), was raised in Stevens Pont, Wisconsin. She has an M.A. in English from the University of South Florida. After years of travel as a military wife, she now lives in Williamsburg, Virginia, with her husband Charles.

Phyllis Hall Haislip lives in Williamsburg where she writes poetry, historical fiction, and nonfiction. Besides writing, she loves being with her family (including her deer family), hiking, and gardening.

Susan Hankla, author of *Clinch River* and *I'm Not Evelyn* (Groundhog Poetry Press), holds a B.A. from Hollins College and an M.F.A. (Creative Writing) from Brown University. She has received the Virginia Prize for Fiction, fellowships to VCCA and the Frost Place, and other recognitions. She lives in Richmond, Virginia.

Warren Meredith Harris, a native Virginian, is the author of several voice plays, one of which was performed on New York City public radio. His poems have appeared in numerous periodicals and in his book *The Night Ballerina* (BrickHouse, 2012). He is the founding editor of *The Clinch Mountain Review.*

Clay Harrison has published over 5,000 poems, four chapbooks, and his memoir, *Wings of Faith.* He was an Army MP, and then served as a police officer in Florida for 32 years, where he wrote numerous poems for celebrities and world leaders. He has lived in Virginia for the past 23 years.

Wendell Hawken lives in the northern Shenandoah Valley where the first meaning of AI is Artificial Insemination. She holds an M.F.A. in Poetry from Warren Wilson College. Her publications include three full poetry collections. A fourth, *After Ward,* was published in May 2022, and a fifth *All About* is scheduled for publication in 2023.

Neva Herrington's *Blue Stone & Other Poems,* one of four published collections, was a Pushcart Foundation "Writer's Choice" selection. Her work has appeared widely in such journals as *The Chariton Review, Southwest Review,* and *The Southern Review.* Having retired from Northern Virginia Community College, Neva moved to Williamsburg in 2017.

Janice Hoffman holds degrees from Indiana University, teaches writing at the post-secondary level, and is published in the US and Canada. Her poetry collections and children's books are on Amazon and Barnes & Noble. She lives in Williamsburg, Virginia. For more information see Facebook at Janice Hoffman Poetry, or her website, jan-hoffman.com.

Ruth Holzer is the author of eight chapbooks, most recently, *Living in Laconia* (Gyroscope Press, 2021) and *Among the Missing* (Kelsay Books, 2021). Her poems have appeared in *Blue Unicorn, Faultline, Slant, Poet Lore, Connecticut River Review*, and *Plainsongs,* among other journals and anthologies. She has received several Pushcart Prize nominations.

Beth Simpson Huddleston has been a Virginia educator for more than 40 years and a member of The Poetry Society of Virginia for more than 35. She has served as Vice President and Director of the Poetry in the Schools Program. She has two sons and five grandchildren, and lives in Winchester, Virginia.

Mark Hudson lives in Evanston, Illinois, and his poetry can be found at Illinoispoets.org. About a year ago, he took a vacation to Williamsburg, Virginia, one that his father planned and which he thoroughly enjoyed. He is happy that one of his poems made it into the anthology.

Luisa A. Igloria, Virginia Poet Laureate, 2020-2022, is the author of 18 poetry collections, including the award-winning *Maps for Migrants and Ghosts.* Originally from Baguio City, Philippines, she teaches Creative Writing and English at Old Dominion University and at The Muse Writers Center. In 2021, the Academy of American Poets awarded her a Poet Laureate Fellowship. Please visit www.luisaigloria.com

Donna Isaac (B.A., M.A., M.F.A.) is a teaching artist/poet, and the author of the poetry book *Footfalls* (Pileated Press, 2018) and three chapbooks: *Tommy, Holy Comforter,* and *Persistence of Vision.* Her work also appears in journals. She serves the literary community in two chapters of the League of Minnesota Poets. Please visit www.donnaisaacpoet.com.

Edison Jennings, the recipient of a Virginia Commission for the Arts Fellowship in Poetry, lives in Abingdon, Virginia, and works as a Head Start bus driver. His poems have appeared in *Boulevard, Kenyon Review, Slate, TriQuarterly,* and elsewhere. Broadstone published his book, *Intentional Fallacies,* in 2021.

Richard Johnson lives in Arlington, Virginia. A graduate of Indiana University (B.A., Germanic Languages; M.S., Education), he has published four full-length poetry collections and numerous poems in various journals. After a tour in Vietnam and West Berlin, he embarked on a career in public service and is now happily retired.

Derek Kannemeyer's writing has appeared in various publications, from *Fiction International* to *Rolling Stone.* His recent books include *Blue Nib #1* (international poetry chapbook contest winner, 2018); *The Play of Gilgamesh* (theater, 2019); *Unsay Their Names* (non-fiction/photography, 2021); *Mutt Spirituals* (San Francisco Bay Press, 2021); and *The Memory Addicts* (a novel, summer 2022).

Robert "Bob" Lester Kelly (1924-2021) held degrees in naval architecture, marine engineering, and industrial management. He and his wife Peggy raised four sons, while he completed an outstanding career designing and building ships for the navy. After retirement he devoted much of his time to poetry, publishing many of his poems in *The Poet's Domain.*

Michael Jon Khandelwal, Executive Director of The Muse Writers Center, a nationally recognized literary center in Norfolk, Virginia, is a teacher and award-winning writer of poetry, fiction, and nonfiction. Michael teaches writing workshops, and he is the current Secretary of the Norfolk Electoral Board and a member of the Norfolk Arts Commission.

JoAnn Lord Koff is the author of *Sand, Pebbles, Fossils, and Rocks* (Sappho Publishing, 2018), a nominee for the Library of Virginia's Literary Award in Poetry, 2019. Her poems appear in numerous journals, among them *InsideNoVA,* where she was Best Author of 2021. She is VP of *Write by the Rails,* and Artist in *ART4US.*

Sarah E. N. Kohrs is an artist and writer, with over 80 journal publications in poetry and photography. She has a teaching license, endorsed in Latin and Visual Arts, homeschools, and creates with clay in her pottery studio. SENK lives in Shenandoah Valley, Virginia, kindling hope amidst asperity. Please see http://senkohrs.com

Carol Parris Krauss's poems are New Southern and appear in a variety of journals, such as *The S.C. Review, Story South,* and *Broadkill Review.* She was honored to be recognized as a Best New Poet by the UVA Press. In 2021, she won the Eastern Shore Writers Association Crossroads Contest.

Carolyn Kreiter-Foronda, Virginia Poet Laureate Emerita, has coedited four anthologies and published ten poetry books, including *The Embrace*, winner of the Art in Literature: The Mary Lynn Kotz Award. Her poems appear in numerous journals, including *Nimrod, Prairie Schooner, Poet Lore, World Poetry Yearbook,* and *Best of Literary Journals.* See www.carolynforonda.com.

After growing up in the wonderful Southern woods, **Robert J. Krieger** attained Eagle Scout, received his Diploma and Degree, then backpacked the Appalachian, Long, and Tuscarora Trails. This inspired him to write and publish his first book of largely outdoor poetry, *Wildflower,* under the pseudonym Jack Patch. Several journeys out West have also sparked his artistic fire.

Joanna Lee's work has been published in *Rattle, Parhelion, Driftwood,* and elsewhere, and nominated for Best of the Net and Pushcart prizes. She is the author of *Dissections* (Finishing Line Press, 2017), co-editor of the anthology *Lingering in the Margins* (Chop Suey Books, 2019), and founder of the Richmond community River City Poets.

Rebecca K. Leet has spent most of her life near the Potomac River and finds that rivers, beaches, and woods open her creative, spiritual world. After a career as a journalist and consultant, she began writing poetry. She is the author of *Living with the Doors Wide Open* (Mercury HeartLink, 2018).

Edward W. Lull has published seven books of poetry, including a historical novel, a memoir, and a textbook, a "how to" book on writing form poetry. He earned a B.S. from the USNA and an M.S. from GWU. He served four terms as president of The Poetry Society of Virginia.

Mike Maggio has published fiction, poetry, and travel reviews in local, national and international publications, including the *Potomac Review* and *Washington City Paper*. His newest collection is *Let's Call It Paradise* (San Francisco Bay Press, 2022). He is a graduate of George Mason University's M.F.A. program in Poetry. His web site is www.mikemaggio.net.

James Irving Mann lives in Charlottesville, Virginia. He grew up in Giles County and graduated from Narrows High School in 1961. He is a former Navy Journalist and was also an English instructor at the Charlottesville branch of the National College of Business and Technology.

Mike McDermott's published works include a chapbook *Reluctant Care* (Finishing Line Press, 2018), and poems in *Quaci Press* (online), *Bourgeon* (online), *Phoebe, Minimus*, and other publications. He holds an M.F.A. degree from George Mason University.

Kindra McDonald, recipient of the 2020 Haunted Waters Press Poetry Award, is the author of *Teaching a Wild Thing*, (Kelsay Books, 2022), *Fossils* (Finishing Line Press, 2019), and *In the Meat Years* (Aldrich Press, 2019). She served as the Vice-President of the PSV Southeastern region (2019-2022). Find her at www. kindramcdonald.com.

A Virginia native, **Anne Metcalf** is a longtime lobbyist for cultural and conservation organizations who rediscovered her childhood love of writing poetry during the pandemic. The mother of three, including a dachshund mix, currently resides in Alexandria.

Alan Meyrowitz retired in 2005 after a career in computer research. His writing has appeared in *Eclectica, Existere, Front Range Review, Inwood Indiana, Jitter, The Literary Hatchet, Lucid Rhythms, The Nassau Review, Poetry Quarterly, Schuylkill Valley Journal, Shark Reef, Shroud, Spirit's Tincture*, and other publications.

Barbara Meyrowitz retired in 2004 after a career in federal acquisition. Her writing has appeared in *Poetry Quarterly, Dark Dossier, Dual Coast Magazine, Nova Bards, Pandemic Magazine, Schuylkill Valley Journal*, and other journals.

Heather Louise Morgan, being mostly gypsy, was surprised to discover her writer's roots here in Virginia. The wonders of nature and wanderlust inform her work. Meditation and yoga help her tap the well where feminism, spirituality, and politics muddy the water.

Susan Notar has flown over Iraq in helicopters wearing body armor, and she makes a mean beurre blanc sauce. Her work has appeared in *Gyroscope, Burningword, Burgeon, The Forgotten River*, and *Antologia de Poemas, Alianza Latina*. She works for the U.S. State Department helping vulnerable communities in the Middle East.

Michelle LT O'Hearn (MiCKi) is a poet/singer/songwriter, born and raised in Virginia. Her artistic resume includes poetry chapbooks, music albums, articles, stage art, contest wins, and multiple journal publications. As a member of The Poetry Society of Virginia and Riverside Writers, MiCKi uses collaborative performances to engage with the community.
See *www.facebook.com/mickiohearn*.

R. L. O'Kelly studied poetry at Rhode Island School of Design and Brown University. His favorite poets then were W. B. Yeats, Dylan Thomas, Hart Crane, and Sylvia Plath. Now retired from academia and government, he prefers to write about issues "close to home" as they are lived, and to probe the mysteries of consciousness and existence.

Nan Ottenritter's chapbook, *Eleanor, Speak*, is available from Finishing Line Press. Her work has appeared in numerous journals, including *Artemis, The New Verse News, Still Point Arts Quarterly, Poets Reading the News*, the *2019 Anthology of The Poetry Society of Virginia*, and *As You Were: The Military Review*.

Marsha Owens's essays and poetry have appeared in *The Sun, Huffington Post, Wild Word Anthology, Dead Mule*, and *Streetlight Anthology*. She is co-editor of the poetry anthology, *Lingering in the Margins*, and her chapbook, *She Watered Her Flowers in the Morning*, is forthcoming from Finishing Line Press.

Linda Kennedy Partee, a late-start poet, developed a passion for writing narrative, historical, philosophical, and memoir poems, often in classical forms. A Williamsburg workshop leader and teacher, Linda has received numerous awards for her poetry, which can be found in a variety of Virginia and California anthologies.

Christian Vincent Pascale published twenty poems in two internationally distributed magazines and authored *Poetry of Wonder* (2021). He also authored a book of short stories, *Memories Are The Stories We Tell Ourselves* (Blue Fortune Enterprises, 2020) and the novel, *The Windows of Heaven* (2022). He served 30 years with the U.S. Government both overseas and domestically. Pascale passed away in Williamsburg, VA on September 18, 2022. See christianpascale.com.

Steven P. Pody's work has been featured in the book *The Panoptikon*, and in numerous anthologies, both in print and on the internet. A military vet, Steven has lived in Alaska, the Middle East, and Africa, and has traveled to 53 countries. He and his wife live in Fredericksburg, Virginia.

Trilla Ramage, a former journalist, is a published and award-winning poet. She lives with her cat in Hampton Roads where she gardens and writes.

Richard L. Rose writes and composes music in Richmond. Recent works are *PushBack*, a poetry collection published by Atmosphere Press in 2021, and *Escape Plans*, an opera.

Anne H. Roseman is a retired librarian who always has a book at the ready (most genres); she is also a Sunday wordsmith and painter, a gardener, and a traveler. Her poems have been published in *Selection*, Winter 1960-61: Chico State College, *The Thomas Nelson Review*, 1982, and *Chico Statements* magazine, Chico Alumni Association, Spring 2013.

David Anthony Sam lives in Virginia with his wife, Linda. Six of his collections are in print. A seventh, *Writing the Significant Soil,* won the Homebound Publications 2021 Poetry Prize and was published in 2022. Sam teaches creative writing at Germanna Community College and serves as Regional Vice-President of The Poetry Society of Virginia.

J.C. Scott's writing focuses on giving voice to the Transgender community, often drawing from personal experiences as a nonbinary writer. She has been published in the *2019 Best Emerging Poets Anthology-Virginia* and is a member of the Hemingway Society, The Poetry Society of Virginia, and the Academy of American Poets.

Leslie Sinclair is a Ph.D. economist, sometime student of the Middle East, and immigrant to the U.S. She wishes to share her education and insight with the wider world, in case some small part of it may be of comfort to others in times of trial.

Kathy Smaltz's poems have been published in numerous journals, and her poetry collection, *Pieces*, was published by Piedmont Press in 2019. A VCCA creative fellow, she served as Prince William County's Poet Laureate from 2016-2018. Married for 25 years, she and her husband have a son in college and three teenagers.

Barbara Drucker Smith is a regional and national anthologized poet and non-fiction writer. Author of *Darling Loraine, the Story of A. Louis Drucker, Prose from the Old Century to the New, A Poetic Journey*, and *A Brush with the Famous*, she received the National Association of Transpersonal Hypnotherapy (NATH) Lifelong Achievement Award in 2020.

Ron Smith, Virginia Poet Laureate Emeritus, has been published in numerous periodicals and anthologies in the U.S., Canada, the U.K., and Italy, including *The Nation, Kenyon Review, New England Review, Georgia Review, Five Points,* and *Arts of War & Peace* (Université Paris Diderot). Among his five volumes is the forthcoming *That Beauty in the Trees.*

Elizabeth Spencer Spragins is a poet, writer, and fiber artist who has contributed to more than 80 journals and anthologies in ten countries. She is the author of three poetry collections: *Waltzing with Water, With No Bridle for the Breeze,* and *The Language of Bones.*

Sofia M. Starnes, D. Litt. (hon.), Virginia Poet Laureate Emerita, is the award-winning author of six poetry collections, including *Fully Into Ashes* (Wings Press, 2011) and *The Consequence of Moonlight* (Paraclete Press, 2018). She is a critique editor and literary translator, and serves on the editorial board of several publications.

Joyce Carr Stedelbauer is a Bible teacher, inspirational speaker, and author of seven books, including her personal journey into widowhood, *A New Widow Learns: Batteries Not Included: Some Assembly Required.* She is a member of the National League of American Pen Women, The Poetry Society of Virginia, and charter member of the Williamsburg Poetry Guild.

Erica Stephens is a Black American poet and performer from Southern Virginia. She graduated from the University of Virginia with a B.A. in Cognitive Neuroscience and Psychology. Her debut collection of poetry is *Black Doves Fly to Freedom* (New Degree Press, 2021).

Judith Stevens, a woods girl, lured into Norfolk by the poet carpenter, teased out of reticence to Open Mics, is finding her voice: persona poems, poems about justice/injustice, poems of growing up in the South, poems about Nature, and poems to lift us a little closer to the Light: You come, too.

Caren Stuart is an award-winning, poet/writer/artist/maker who lives in Chatham County, NC, with her very supportive husband. As sole proprietor of "convoluted notions," she designs, creates, and sells all manner of art, jewelry, and craft. Her writing appears in *Shot Glass Journal, Redheaded Stepchild, Kakalak,* and many other publications.

Beverly Jo Subudhi was born in Detroit and graduated from Wayne State University with a B.F.A. in Painting/Printmaking. She was a Library Associate (reference section) at Bon Air Library for 25 years. Besides writing and reading, she enjoys spending time with her four children and seven grandchildren—and swimming laps.

Martha Thomas Terrell, a native Californian, relocated to Williamsburg, Virginia, over forty years ago to attend William & Mary and embrace her Tidewater family roots. After a thirty-year professional career at W&M, she retired to write, the fulfillment of a dream she has had since the 3rd grade.

Jenna Villforth Veazey currently resides in Virginia and is the author of a chapbook of poems, *The Rise of Jennifer*. Her poetry has been published in *The Fredericksburg Literary and Arts Review* as well as *Baby Bug Magazine* and *Highlights High Five*. She is a member of the Water Street Writers and a certified Virginia Master Naturalist.

Drury Wellford is a native of Richmond, VA. She lived for many years in New York City, followed by stints in Mexico City and Buenos Aires, and a few places in between. These varied experiences have been the inspirations that led to her journey of self-expression through poetry.

Erin Newton Wells is a teacher with a background in the visual arts, languages, and writing. She has received numerous awards for poetry, including the Sow's Ear Prize, judged by Jericho Brown. Her work appears in *Barrow Street*, *Spillway*, *Poetry South*, *Rattle*, and *Sow's Ear Review*, among other publications. She lives in Charlottesville, Virginia.

Frederick Wilbur is an architectural woodcarver and has written three books on the subject. His poetry collections are *As Pus Floats the Splinter Out* (Kelsay Books, 2018) and *Conjugation of Perhaps* (Main Street Rag, 2020). He is poetry co-editor for *Streetlight Magazine* (online).

Denise Wilcox lives in Keswick, VA. She is an award-winning author who writes poetry and nonfiction for all ages. Her work has been published in *Paterson Literary Review*, *Ladybug*, *Fun for Kidz Magazine*, *Quilted Poems*, *Highlighter* (the journal of the Society for Children's Book Writers and Illustrators), and *Developmental Medicine and Child Neurology Journal*.

Beth Oast Williams has published poetry in *West Texas Literary Review*, *Wisconsin Review*, *Glass Mountain*, *GASHER Journal*, *Poetry South*, *Fjords Review*, and *Rattle's* Poets Respond, among other publications. Her poems have been nominated twice for the Pushcart Prize. Her first chapbook, *Riding Horses in the Harbor*, was published by Finishing Line Press in 2020.

Kristie L. Williams received degrees from SAPC and ECU. Her chapbook, *Finding Her*, was published by Finishing Line Press in August 2022. She plays with words, using her own story of quadriplegia and cerebral palsy to advocate for herself and others with disabilities, while creating mixed media art.

Diana Woodcock's book, *Facing Aridity* (Homebound Publications/Wayfarer Books, 2021), was a finalist for the 2020 Prism Prize for Climate Literature. *Holy Sparks* (Paraclete Poetry Prize finalist, 2020) is forthcoming in 2023. Recipient of the 2011 Vernice Quebodeaux Pathways Poetry Prize for Women for *Swaying on the Elephant's Shoulders*, Woodcock currently teaches at VCUarts Qatar.

Katherine E. Young, Arlington, Virginia, inaugural Poet Laureate (2016-2018) and editor of *Written in Arlington*, is the author of *Woman Drinking Absinthe* (Alan Squire Publishing, 2020) and *Day of the Border Guards* (University of Arkansas Press, 2014). She has translated numerous Russian-language writers and was named a 2017 NEA Translation Fellow.

Laura Younger resides in Alexandria, VA, working as a government plod and scribbling in her spare time. Her poetry has appeared in *Artemis Journal, Kakalak,* and various anthologies from *Old Mountain Press.*

Sally Zakariya's poetry has been nominated for the Pushcart Prize and Best of the Net. Her publications include *When You Escape* (2016), *Personal Astronomy* (2018), *Muslim Wife* (2019), *The Unknowable Mystery of Other People* (2019), and *Something Like a Life* (2021). She edited and designed a poetry anthology, *Joys of the Table*, and blogs at www.butdoesitrhyme.com.

The Poetry Society of Virginia
Centennial Anthology
Appendix D
Acknowledgments

"Near to You" by Obelia Akanke first appeared in *Tried and Tested: Heart of Crystal (Book Two)* (2019).

"Snowdrop in the Supermarket at Midnight" by April J. Asbury first appeared in *The Anthology of Appalachian Writers* (2013).

"The True Story of Eric's Head" by April J. Asbury first appeared in *Woman With Crows* (Finishing Line Press, 2021).

"Short Order" by Bill Ayres first appeared in *Blue Collar Review* (2021).

"Far Side of the Moon" by Zeina Azzam first appeared in in *Bayna Bayna, In-Between,* 2021.

"Hugging the Tree" by Zeina Azzam first appeared in *Streetlight Magazine.*

"Collapse of the Silver Bridge" and "Brown-Eyed World" by Madalin Jackson Bickel first appeared in *Some Kind of Alternate Universe* (2016).

"Perpetuities," "Tour Guide, Rhine River Cruise," and "Little Thanksgivings" by Patsy Anne Bickerstaff first appeared in *The Cloak*, the monthly publication of St. Martin's Church, Richmond, Virginia.

"The Girl Who Could Not Decide," "Dear God, You Made Me Too Short," and "The Unfortunate Beetle" by Laura J. Bobrow first appeared in her chapbook *A Little Bit of Banter* (Limited Distribution).

"Darling of Darkness," "They Don't Make Forever Like They Used To," and "Leaving Fourth Street" by Kenneth F. Conklin first appeared in *The Zen of Ken,* (Cyberwit, 2021).

"Mrs. Creekmore's May Peas" by Pamela Brothers Denyes first appeared in the *Journal of the Virginia Writers Club* (2021).

"Honest as Open Wind" and "What to Carry With You" by Pamela Brothers Denyes first appeared in *The Right Mistakes* (2022).

"Daughter of the Mountains" by Sharon Canfield Dorsey first appeared in her book *Tapestry* (High Tide Publications, 2016).

"Summer Leaves the Hills" and "Love is a Perfect Pineapple" by Sharon Canfield Dorsey first appeared in her book *Walk With Me* (High Tide Publications, 2020).

"God's Cathedral" by John L. Dutton II first appeared in the *Journal of the Virginia Writers Club Golden Nib* (2020).

"Home" by John L. Dutton II first appeared in the *Journal of the Virginia Writers Club Golden Nib* (2021).

"Walking My Human" by John L. Dutton II first appeared in *NoVa Bards Anthology* (2020).

"Song of the Cynic" by Catherine Fletcher first appeared in *Eunoia Review* (Singapore, 2016).

"Didelphis Virginiana" by Rich Follett first appeared in *poetic diversity - the poetry zine of los angeles* (April, 2019).

"peeper paean" by Rich Follett first appeared in *The Bryce Mountain Courier* (2014).

"Lobstering at 96" by Eric J. Forsbergh first appeared in *Passager Journal* (Winter, 2020).

"On a Surgeon Poet" by Eric J. Forsbergh first appeared in *The Journal of the American Medical Association* (June, 2019).

"Bestiary" by Chapman Hood Frazier first appeared in *The Southern Poetry Review* (2021).

"Crow" by Chapman Hood Frazier first appeared in *The Orchards Poetry Journal* (2018).

"Owlets" by Chapman Hood Frazier first appeared in *Triggerfish Critical Review* (July, 2022).

"The Lone Merganser" by Greg Friedmann first appeared in *Poetry Virginia, Collected Poems by The Poetry Society of Virginia* (2019).

"At Hickory Hill, July 30,1864" by Sue Davis Gabbay first appeared in her chapbook *Through the Archway* (2021).

"The Guesser" by James L. Garrett first appeared in *The Journal* of The Writer's Guild of Virginia (Fall-Winter, 2021).

"Catheter Ablation" by Claudia Gary first appeared in *Brazen Head* (UK, 2021).

"Balloon Flowers, Memorial Day" by Claudia Gary first appeared in *Trinacria* (2015), and is also included in her chapbook *Let's Get Out of Here* (Loudoun Scribe, 2015).

"Aunt Rose" by Claudia Gary first appeared in *The Rotary Dial* (2015).

"Dark Matter" by Bill Glose first appeared in *Golden Laureates Anthology* (2022).

"Theories of Flight and Forbearance" by Bill Glose first appeared in *The Missouri Review* (2016).

"Orison" by Marjorie Gowdy first appeared in *Floyd County Moonshine* (Fall, 2021).

"Cloudy Day" by Lyman Grant first appeared in *Equinox* (2021).

"Passage through the Sinks" by Cathy Hailey first appeared in *Poetry Virginia Review* (2016), reprinted in *Confetti*.

"A Doll and a Dream" by Cathy Hailey first appeared in *Stay Salty: Life in the Garden State*, Vol. 2. (2021).

"Wind and River" by Cathy Hailey first appeared in *NoVA Bards* (2020).

"Stepping out" and "Without Brakes" by Mary Mallek Haines first appeared in her poetry collection *Beads of an Abacus* (San Francisco Bay Press, 2011).

"A Game Board" by Mary Mallek Haines first appeared in *The William and Mary Review* (2015).

"Theology at Eighty Miles an Hour" by Warren Meredith Harris first appeared in *The Hampden-Sydney Poetry Review* (2003).

"Dylan's Places" by Warren Meredith Harris first appeared in *Candelabrum Poetry Magazine* (UK) (2004).

"Haiku for the Metrorail" by Warren Meredith Harris was carved around the base of a monumental sculpture outside the Spring Hill Station of the Washington, D.C. Metrorail (2016).

"Boston Strong" by Clay Harrison, winner of the Reader's Choice Award, first appeared in the *Daily Press* (2013).

"Peace" by Clay Harrison, winner of the Reader's Choice Award, first appeared in the *Daily Press* (2015).

"Within the Confines of this Pasture, How the Universe is Understood" by Wendell Hawken first appeared in *The Luck of Being* (2008).

"Question" by Wendell Hawken first appeared in *White Bird* (2017).

"Aubade" by Wendell Hawken first appeared in *Calyx, A Journal of Art and Literature by Women* (2020).

"Breakdown with Starlings" by Neva Herrington first appeared in *Blue Stone & Other Poems,* Still Point Press (1986); reprinted in *Among the Absent: New and Selected Poems,* Finishing Line Press (2019).

"Namesake" by Neva Herrington first appeared in *Her BMW and Other Poems,* Pudding House Publications Chapbook Series (2008); reprinted in *Open Season,* David Robert Books (2015); reprinted in *Among the Absent: New and Selected Poems,* Finishing Line Press (2019).

"A Family Chair" by Neva Herrington first appeared in *Open Season,* David Robert Books, (2015); reprinted in *Among the Absent: New and Selected Poems,* Finishing Line Press (2019).

"Cargoes" by Luisa A. Igloria first appeared in *Swwim Miami* (March 19, 2019) https://www.swwim.org/blog/2019/3/13/cargoes.

"Bioluminescence" by Luisa A. Igloria first appeared in Issue 12 of ONE (Jacar Press) http://one.jacarpress.com/issue-12/#Luisa%20A.%20Igloria.

"Custody" by Luisa A. Igloria first appeared in Poem-a-Day, by the Academy of American Poets (March 19, 2021) https://poets.org/poem/custody?msclkid=238f6a04a88c11ecb1a8cfaa987f5ad3.

"Directions to a Ruin" by Edison Jennings first appeared in *Sow's Ear Poetry Review* (2002).

"Spontaneous Combustion" by Edison Jennings first appeared in *Anthology of Southern Poetry, Volume III, Appalachia* (2011).

"Cold Spring Morning and the Grade School" by Edison Jennings first appeared in *Rattle* (2021).

"Cartagena Excursion" by Richard Johnson first appeared in *Haunted Waters,* online (2020).

"Emigrant," by Michael Jon Khandelwal, first appeared in *Port Folio Weekly* (January 9, 2007).

"Hay Elote," by Michael Jon Khandelwal, first appeared in *Rattle* (June 1, 2008).

"Illuminations on Ocracoke Ferry" by JoAnn Lord Koff first appeared in *Sand, Pebbles, Fossils, and Rocks* (Sappho Publishing, 2018); reprinted in *The Art of Everyone* (2021).

"So" by JoAnn Lord Koff first appeared in *Black Bough Poetry's Freedom-Rapture* (2021).

"Tinnitus" by Carolyn Kreiter-Foronda first appeared in *Delaware Poetry Review;* reprinted in *These Flecks of Color: New and Selected Poems,* San Francisco Bay Press (2018).

"Red Flecks on a Veneer of Black" by Sarah E. N. Kohrs first appeared in *Scintilla Magazine,* (2018).

"Into the Depths" by Sarah E. N. Kohrs first appeared in *Horn & Ivory Zine* (2017).

"Crossing at Culpeper" by Robert J. Krieger, is excerpted from his poetry collection *Wildflower: Adventures of a Warrior,* published under the pen name, Jack Patch, Mountain Arbor Press (2021).

"Small Mercies" by Joanna Lee first appeared in *Dissections*, Finishing Line Press (2017).

"Ebb Tide" by Rebecca K. Leet first appeared in *Passager* (2018).

"Where Giants Walked" by Edward W. Lull first appeared in *Where Giants Walked,* Infinity Publishing (2005).

"The New Dominion" by Edward W. Lull first appeared in *Creating Form Poetry,* Infinity Publishing (2013).

"Called to Serve" by Edward W. Lull first appeared in *The Reality and Fantasy of My World,* High Tide Publications, Inc. (2017).

"The Master Fitter's Apprentice" by Mike Maggio first appeared in *The Northern Virginia Review*, Volume 26 (Spring, 2012).

"Iris of Spring" by Mike Maggio first appeared in *The Paragon Journal* (November 15, 2017).

"Creation is Calling" by James Irving Mann first appeared in the *Newsletter of the Creation Spirituality Communities*, Carlsbad, California 92008 (Sep/Oct, 2021).

"Could we Live?" by Kindra McDonald first appeared in *Headline Poetry and Press* (2020).

"Breaking" by Alan Meyrowitz first appeared in *Existere* (Spring/Summer, 2013).

"Night Lilies" by Alan Meyrowitz first appeared in *Forge* (Winter, 2011-2012).

"A Whisper Is" by Barbara Meyrowitz first appeared in *Nova Bards Anthology* (2021).

"Botanica" by Susan Notar first appeared in *Gyroscope,* Issue 21-1 (Winter, 2021).

"Yezidi, Northern Iraq" by Susan Notar first appeared in *Burningword Literary Journal* (April, 2021).

"Creating a Green Scene" by Michelle LT O'Hearn (MiCKi) first appeared in *The Poet's Domain*, Vol. 26 (2010).

"The Light in April" by R.L. O'Kelly first appeared in *A Commonwealth of Poetry,* the PSV Newsletter (April, 2014).

"The Lost Country" by R.L. O'Kelly first appeared in *A Commonwealth of Poetry,* the PSV Newsletter (September, 2014).

"Little Lincoln" by Nan Ottenritter first appeared in *Poetry Virginia: Collected Poems from The Poetry Society of Virginia* (2019); reprinted in *Eleanor, Speak: Poems by Nan Ottenritter*, Finishing Line Press (2021).

"Of Place" by Nan Ottenritter first appeared in *Still Point Arts Quarterly,* published by Shanti Arts LLC (2021).

"Gypsum Dunes" by Christian Vincent Pascale won 2nd place in the Chesapeake Bay Writers Golden Nib contest (2021).

"Ghosts at the Table" by Christian Vincent Pascale first appeared in *Poetry of Wonder,* Blue Fortune Enterprises LLC (2021).

"Her Room Upstairs" by Christian Vincent Pascale first appeared in *Songs in the Night,* Blue Fortune Enterprises LLC (2022).

"East Virginia" by Steven P. Pody first appeared in the online poetry sites, Booksie.com and AllPoetry.com.

"On Wings of Dappled Clarity" by Steven P. Pody first appeared in the nature journal quarterly *The Avocet* (Summer, 2021), as well as in Booksie.com and AllPoetry.com.

"Backyard Philosophy" by Anne H. Roseman first appeared in *Quilted Poems: An Ekphrastic Collaboration of Poets and Quilters*, BookBaby (2022).

"Gypsy Woman" and "Roosevelt Lake" by Kathy Smaltz first appeared in her collection of poetry, *Pieces*, PJPF Press (2019).

"Declaiming" by Ron Smith first appeared in *The Georgia Review*; reprinted in his collection *Running Again in Hollywood Cemetery* (MadHat Press, 2nd edition, 2019).

"Its Ghostly Workshop" by Ron Smith first appeared in *Blackbird* as "Advice to My Grandson"; reprinted in *Its Ghostly Workshop* (LSU Press, 2013).

"Photograph of Jesse Owens at the Gun" by Ron Smith first appeared in *Arete*; reprinted in *Running Again in Hollywood Cemetery* (MadHat Press, 2nd edition, 2019).

"Songs of the Southern Rim" by Elizabeth Spencer Spragins first appeared in *Time of Singing*, Vol. 47, No. 2 (Summer, 2020).

"What Trees Remember" by Elizabeth Spencer Spragins first appeared in *The Orchards Poetry Journal* (Summer, 2020).

"Baptism of Desire" by Sofia M. Starnes first appeared in *Spiritus* (2015); reprinted in *The Consequence of Moonlight,* Paraclete Press (2018).

"Why Honeymoons are Brief" by Sofia M. Starnes first appeared in *A! A Magazine for the Arts* (2014); reprinted in *The Consequence of Moonlight,* Paraclete Press (2018).

"The Soul's Landscape" by Sofia M. Starnes first appeared in *Pavement Saw Magazine* (2002); reprinted in *A Commerce of Moments*, Pavement Saw Press (2003, 2nd edition, 2013).

"In the Beginning…" and "Jamestown Musings" by Joyce Carr Stedelbauer first appeared in *Batteries Not Included,* High Tide Publications (2021).

"The Rose of Hope" by Erica Stephens first appeared in *Black Doves Fly to Freedom*, New Degree Press (2021).

"I Am Not Spew Marrow Creek" by Caren Stuart first appeared in *Kakalak*, Main Street Rag Publishing Company (2015).

"Prosthesis" by Beverly Jo Subudhi won 1st Place in the Cenie Moon Memorial Contest, sponsored by The Poetry Society of Virginia. The poem first appeared in *Poetry Virginia,* Wider Perspectives Publishing (2020).

"Levitate," "High Definition," and "Your Hand at Work" by Martha Thomas Terrell first appeared on the author's blog, WordShelter.com.

"Lunar Howling" by Drury Wellford first appeared in *Artemis*, Vol. XXVII (2021).

"A Simple Asking" by Frederick Wilbur first appeared in *Artemis Journal*, Volume XXII (2015); reprinted in *As Pus Floats the Splinter Out*, Kelsay Books (2018).

"Among Stones" by Frederick Wilbur first appeared in *The Midwest Quarterly*, Volume 62, (2020); reprinted in *Conjugation of Perhaps*, Main Street Publishing Company (2020).

"Kickball" by Beth Oast Williams first appeared in *GASHER* Journal (July, 2020).

"I Knew Better Than to Say" by Beth Oast Williams first appeared in *Rattle's* Poets Respond, (January 10, 2021).

"Driving to Juniata" by Katherine E. Young first appeared in *qarrtsiluni*.

"The Bear" by Katherine E. Young first appeared in *Prairie Schooner;* reprinted in her collection *Woman Drinking Absinthe*, Alan Squire Publishing (2021).

"Star Light, Star Bright" by Sally Zakariya first appeared in *Bourgeon* (May 29, 2021).

"Missing the Lunar Eclipse" by Sally Zakariya first appeared in *Soundings East* (Spring, 2022).

www.ingramcontent.com/pod-product-compliance
Lightning Source LLC
Chambersburg PA
CBHW041554010826
48981CB00052B/573/J